A

The SkullFuck Collection

Jeremy Void

Other books by Jeremy Void

Derelict America

Nefarious Endeavors

Smash a Lightbulb
Poetry for Lowlifes

Erase Your Face:
The SkullFuck Collection

Just a Kid

Sex Drugs & Violence:
Incomplete Stories for the Incomplete Human

An Art Form:
The Crass Poetry Collection

My Story:
The Short Version

I Need Help:
The SkullFuck Collection

The Lost Letters

Chaos Writing

The TR*TH

My Psychedelic Suicide

Spoken word albums by Jeremy Void

Absurd Nihilism

Word Vomit

A Crass Philosophy

The SkullFuck Collection

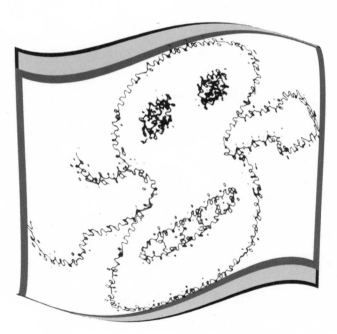

JeremyVoid

A Crass Philosophy: The SkullFuck Collection

ISBN Number:
978-0-578-18307-7

ChaosWriting *Press*

IT'S A MINDFUCK
www.chaoswriting.net

To All Those Who Try To Censor US
This one's for you!

"No artist tolerates
reality"

— Friedrich Nietzsche

My mission statement

Don't you dare say I need spirituality!

cuz I'm a Buddhist

and I'm really into zen philosophy.

Don't you dare tell me I'm sick!

because I am,

it's common knowledge;
no need to point out the obvious.

Don't you dare point your finger at me
and tell me I'm wrong!

because anyone who believes in anything

is usually wrong,
is the way that it goes.

You see, my mission, my goal as a writer, is to show you that we're all corrupt, every last one of us. The human race is sick and anyone who claims to be any different is only fooling themselves. I say

embrace your insanity
embrace your crazy side   because we only die once!

I think art is a very important component of anyone's life. Whether or not the art is any good and someone might wanna buy it is unimportant. What's important is that I'm using my mind for the greater good. I'm actively exercising my brain which is something so few of us do by choice. Plus, I'm creating something new, and for that, regardless of the quality, is something special and beautiful. Just the fact that we have a brain, free-will, and the gift of creation is something to cherish, don't you think?

IT STARTS HERE

IT STARTS HERE

If you're not offended
then I haven't done right by you

3

This I know

I don't know anything. I could pretend to know something but that would only end in shame and disappointment. I know nothing, I have no answers, and I prefer to keep it that way. I am just another spec in a universe of shit, I can't possibly begin to imagine the innerworkings of things. I don't preach, I don't like preachers; I don't lecture, I hate lecturers. I try to remain neutral in all things politics. Some would call that apathetic, but I call some shit. I'm a nihilist, I guess I do know that. I do know that I know nothing. I am only a man. I am not a god. People who think they know are full of shit. Sometimes I too think I know, I'll admit, but what I think I know is that I too am full of shit. But I prefer it that way....

Attack of the
I-Slaves

Based on a true story

I am not like ordinary men. I think in a way that makes the mass populous shudder. My thoughts and dreams are banned from most libraries, my ideas and schemes forbidden from any text book. I'm just a human being trying to navigate my way through a world crammed tight with let-downs and set-backs. I write because I need to, not because I want to, but there's a magic beneath the pen as it scrawls word for word, as I scribble my internal drama between the lines. It's almost like giving birth, painful to let it out, but boy does it feel good that it will fester inside you no longer, and now you can raise and nourish it. That's a magical thing, isn't it?

by Jeremy Void

Words are my weapon

If you piss me off, I will **MURDER YOU**

I COULD break it to you nicely,

and I would

But if you piss me off, then **I WONT!**

8

# The Serenade

I thought I heard something that made me high
it made me hot
You see I'm a nervous kid only I'm 28,
stripped of pills that made me calm.
Stripped of drugs which made me cool.
Stripped of life as I kissed the moon.

I lived fast and slow, cold and hot
I just don't know.
I can't get these words to flow when
I talk, but I **know** The Words and I can **use** The Words
to blow you away.

I'll make you high
I'll make you hot
Come with me and we'll
rob the lot.
Let's dance together beneath the moon
rip off our skin and get real crude.

I don't speak of sex
I don't speak of appeal
I don't speak of recklessness
I speak of real.

I speak of you and I on the kill
I speak of you and I getting thrills
I speak of you and I running around aimlessly
I speak of the sky melting as the stars shine bright and sick.

What do you say? A single night
you and I in the raw.
A single night of chills and we'll be biting
and scratching as roosters squeal.

I don't speak of sex
I don't speak of appeal
I don't speak of being
just another lover
cuz I want your number and
we can go from there.

All I speak of is
you and I and one night
you'll simply never forget.

I am a human being
no more
no less

I feel a multitude of emotions

Some enjoy the darker stuff because it gives them something to relate to

Some enjoy the brighter stuff because it pulls them out of the dirty water people typically find themselves knee-deep in when they take an honest look around them

GET YOUR HEADS OUT OF YOUR ASSES

because this is me
this is who I am I am a human being
no more ⟶ no less

The Beginning Of The End

Dear Paper

Dear Paper
What the hell do you
want from me?
Isn't this enough?
I mean, I
filled up your lines,
with words
now didn't I?

Dear Paper
for weeks I've been
staring at a blank screen
just waiting for
the words to come out of me
    but it's
      no use

What else do you want?
I fed you
I treated you with
upmost respect
and all I get
is a freaking blank screen
in return....

I'm stuck
and I have
nothing to say anymore.

And now I'm done
and now it's over
and I'm stuck

Dear Paper
dear paper, won't you
relieve me of
this state of being before I
go apeshit and murder someone....

Dear paper
please give me a
sign
give me a prompt
to trigger something
exciting
but nothing exciting
happens here
    ever

I'm a writer for pete's sake
and words, they heal me
stitch up the rage that would otherwise
flow right out of me
and swallow some
unsuspecting ASSHOLE
whole——
      I could only hope....

Dear Paper
deliver me

    PLEASE

12

I apologize if I rant here, because I got so much on my mind. I'm not good at staying sober and I hate myself and my life and everyone in my life and most of all, I hate me, me, me, because I'm fucking crazy and out of my mind, and no one gets me, especially in Rutland, because I like thnigs loud and fast and chaotic and fast, and if things aren't that way, I get even crazier, and that's why the music I listen to is fast; it simply calms me down. And everyone is pushing me to slow down and chill out but that doesn't work for me because now I don't know my ass from my head, and up is down and left is right and I'm so fucking assbackwards all the time because their life isn't for me, and they're trying to squeeze a square peg in a round hole, and the more they smash it to fit, the more it dings and dents and chips apart, and all they're going to end up with is a deformed square that isn't even a shape anymore, but a misshapen block. And that's me and that's how I feel right now, and I don't know anything about getting sober because I can't seem to get that right. A girl at the AA meeting today cried because she was so depressed and I said to her at least she can cry, because I forgot how to do that a really long time ago, but I'm fucking crying right now. I went to my therapist and showed him this story because I was really proud of it, getting all my shit out there, and he said it's gonna scare people and they'll think I'm a monster but I am a fucking monster and I don't give a fuck what they think and if it scares people, then fuck em because that's how things were for me and it wasm't pretty, none of it was, and if they're scared, they will know how it is to be me.

Before My Eyes

What's the meaning of life?
I find myself asking when the wakes
even out to a minute shifting.
My pondering strengthens and then
the rush of water heightens to an epic surge
that pulls my focus away from the prior
ruminations that only serve to make me mad.

I sit on a ledge
staring out yonder, watching
as the pigs are fed
the birds have fled
and I wonder briefly
what it means
to be dead.

Life is like a puppet
we use it till it breaks.
Like a computer
pressing buttons till
it quakes.

I'm frequently finding myself bored
lost
angry   and wasteful
wasted
washed up on the beach that lies
in the middle of denial.

No options left
in this fragment of a dream.
I sit here and try
trying my hardest
just to fall asleep.

The bats flutter and dive.
They rise and flicker in the night.
I watch them in dark flashes
free to be fast and wild.
I wonder what it would be like
to have that kind of power
to be that kind of liberated.
but only in a dream will it ever come to be

I sit here on an island
watching as the boats
slue through and about.
I watch them stammer over
waves and steady when the rolling
deadens.

My life is crumbling
to a million and one pieces.
I tried AA meetings to
piece it back together,
but the attempt has backfired

and now I'm sober
with no place to go.

only I just can't fall asleep

so I sit here and I watch....

15

No, he's a queer playing Punk rock. But to me Punk rock was never a game, it was life or death. Not something I could just walk away from when my friends turned on me, when that mixed martial arts coach held me by my throat at the convenient store threatening to murder me and smashed my head again and again on the pavement—I could not just step out of my skin, step out of my spikey leather jacket, step out of my stretch jeans; all those littles symbols and slogans that you and I know so well and which tainted every piece of fabric I ever put over my skin, I could not just leave it all behind—just step into my Punk rock clothing at the Punk rock show where everyone else is going along with it too and dressing up and this Punk rock way of life fits in so perfectly here, so nice and right, but then step out of it right before the cops slam me against the brick wall under the bridge. It was more than just a fashion to me, more than a game, a gimmick, a romantic sensation that seemed appealing from the outside view, it was more than anything I could ever use to describe it. In short, it was my home. I went to it when I was angry, I went to it when I was sad. It always knew the right thing to say to make me feel better, to lift my spirits, make me feel like I'm not such a fuckup after all—no, wait, it made me feel like even more of a fuckup than I already felt I was. It told me there's nothing wrong with that, be proud of who I am, cuz if I'm a fuckup I've gotta spend the rest of my life in this skin and I might as well be proud of my defects, my follies, wear my failures like a badge of honor. See, that's what Shane West lacks. He's a movies star, although I heard he came to California originally to be in a Punk band and ended up as an actor anyway. But even so, that desire to be in a Punk band is what makes him not Punk at all. My theory is, anyone can play Punk, it's not that hard to do. But in the '70s and '80s nobody wanted to play Punk—and I mean nobody. So that weeded out all the non-Punks. If you played Punk chances are it wasn't some dream of yours to star in a Punk band; chances are, you just failed at everything else you'd ever done and this was your last hope to do something real with your life. Punk rock was all I had, it was all you had I'm taking it, it was all a lot of us had; but in this day and age, with movies like SLC Punk floating around, Punk becomes cool. Punk becomes romantic, a sensation. But I'll tell you this, being Punk is not pretty and it's not romantic. Sure, there were the fun times like surfing a wave of extended hands or busting your knee pretty badly in a mosh pit while the Business played, but then there were the bad times too, like getting beat down, locked up, and kicked around, and for me I had no other choice. I see these Punk kids today who are COOL—and they come from pampered lives and they roll with the jocks and preps and metal heads and anyone else who will accept them—which is everybody. I despise the pampered Punks, I'll hate them till the day I die. And do you know why?—of course you do—it's because they're mocking my lifestyle, they're parading around in the very thing that I hold so dearly to my terminally deformed heart, the very thing that had brought me through year after year of misery and pain; they're fucking my girlfriend and prancing around saying, *Hey Jeremy, I just fucked your girlfriend,* and then going to the next person, *Hey Frank, I just fucked Jeremy's girlfriend,* and so on. It's disprespectful to call yourself Punk but not know a goddamn thing about what that represents. It's just another silly rich kid game, another counterculture for the rich to exploit. These kids got their teeth into everything, and I wanna sink my teeth into them. See how they like it.

Didn't slip this time.

Jeremy Void: 03
Ice: 542

Insightful Segment from
Chaos Writing:

An Existential Funk

I've been in an existential funk that probably started a few months ago, but has evolved since then. I've been thinking a lot about people, or more specifically, me in regards to people. There are so many of us on this earth, all with our own agendas, stories, interests, personalities, etc. And yet—I am me, stuck as me, forever doomed to this shell of a body that is mine. It's not that I'm unhappy with myself—or maybe I am a little—but that being stuck in a single body is just so inhibiting. I want to know more, to be more; I don't want to be human anymore. I want to experience life through another set of eyes; I want to remember a past that isn't mine.

Only Time Will Tell

The past is a puzzle
that keeps coming back to me.
The pieces materialize before me.
   My sanity
   My life
The whole world revolves
around   everyone
but me,
     and I know this now.
     I know this now.
     I know I'm not
number one anymore....   (it was the hardest thing to
   grasp.)

—   —   —   —

People I used like Chess pieces
Today I know them by name
Tomorrow we might be friends
   ....Who knows?
As soon as I get rid of my resentments
As soon as I
give up the fight
   it will all come back.
   in time it'll all come back.
The future will come together
become the present
and we can go from there...

In a world filled to the brink with filthy politicians I've gotta stand tall, stand above, do my best to not get lost in their rhetoric, their rhetorical rubbish—I wipe my ass with it. I live alone in my apartment where I'm immersed in books and fruit flies (but those are another story)—and I don't watch the news, read the newspaper, get lost in the tabloids, I just don't fucking care who's fucking who—politics is really just an orgy, don't you know? He fucked she, she fucked he, they all fucked each other in their oh so homoerotic white house—I'd love to spray-paint a swastika on that, a hammer-and-sickle to support the commie turds (Che Guevara would be very proud to see that his hard work had paid off and some-body still cares about his cause, but fuck Che Guevara, he was a preacher, a pseudo-revolutionary, who had achieved nothing—and besides, I happen to like Capitalism). Fuck them all and drown them in their own wasted existences. Hang them up and beat em with an inch of their lives—just to hear the truth, that's all I want from them.

But in a world where everything is fabricated by Facebook, is truth a real entity, or a demon of the past? Did truth ever exist to begin with? You got '80s punks screaming about how they want the truth. You got '70s punks screaming that they've had enough of the lie. In the '60s there were hippies without clothing wandering around high on acid saying they want the truth. (What truth? You're an acid head, you wouldn't know the truth if it pissed on your hairy face.)

So what's the point if there are no truths? Well, except for those of Facebook and Wikipedia, because any idiot with a computer can speak their opinion on just about any subject. (Thank you very much, Social Media. As a result of your totally selfless kindness I'm getting reamed out by guys who couldn't even write themselves out of a paper bag, who think they have the merits to hassle me about my own writing.)

Just remember kids
when push comes to shove
when the shit hits the fan
when the crowd scrambles and runs
for cover, just remember this:

There are no truths anymore
There are no lies
Everything's equivalent
No one's right
Everyone's wrong
It's a fact

Feel free to check my sources on that. They're legit.

WORKS CITED:

Facebook
Wikipedia
Deviant Art

Most people are confined to a box,
and anything outside of said box
requires an explanation or else the
person doesn't believe it exists.

AND I"M SICK OF EXPLAINING

The TR*TH

Introducing The TR*TH

I'm sober, I'm happy——but I'm lonely, and at times I feel so utterly drab as if all hope is depleting me, and soon I'll be stuck in a nihilistic sea of angst and frustration. . . .

But don't get me wrong, I like being sober, I like this life, I like being here, and if I wasn't me, but someone else, I'd be even worst off, I suppose.

So all this bitching and moaning from me is just what I have to do to vent at times, to let out my frustration so that it doesn't burrow deep inside me and bob its head out at the worst possible moment——

and you all know what would happen then, right?

I CAN
PISS FARTHER THAN YOU

Insightful Segment from
Chaos Writing:

Interpreting Poetry

You cannot teach a writer how to write!
You cannot teach an artist how to paint or draw!
Nor can a photographer learn how to snap shots of the world!

It must come from inside....
      education only standardizes
      and art cannot be standardized unless
      it's generic and boring ....
      commercialized crap/// Teachers teach you

how to fall in line, how to follow the rules,
how to read poetry the way they deem fit.
              See what I'm getting at here?

25

Jeremy Void,   who is your favorite poet?

It used to be Richard Hell, you know, the bassist of Television, the original singer of the Heartbreakers (not Tom Petty and the Fartbreaker, no; I'm talking the REAL Heartbreakers, the only Heartbreakers that broke my heart when the singer died of a heroin overdose all those years ago (R.I.P.)—you know, Johnny Thunders. Richard Hell was the original singer and then he broke loose and started up the Voidoids, which I think are better anyway, and then Johnny Thunders moved in to the Heartbreakers like a greedy pirate and sang such lovely songs as "Born to Lose"; songs as miraculous and devastatingly honest and terribly brilliant as "Pirate Love" and "All By Myself" and many more classics from his album *LAMF*, which stands for "Like a Motherfucker."
But back to Richard Hell. He was my favorite poet way back when—keyword, "was," as in past-tense—when I was much less experienced with the underground world of art and literature (but don't get me wrong, I still hold his writing and his music and his everything else that made him RICHARD HELL very close to my heart, for his music was the perfect soundtrack for a drug-fueled existence like my own; and his written work was like an open book depicting the mess in which I exist day in and day out—you know what I'm talking about: that narcissistic wasteland that all great artists find themselves in when they take an honest look at their lives and for the first time ever realize that they are all alone—so alone it's both sad and titillating and so detrimentally marvelous and scary too that it gives me a hard-on just to think about it.) Anyway, where was I?
JUST SO YOU KNOW, I HAVE NOT SLEPT IN OVER SEVENTY-TWO HOURS BECAUSE I FIND I'M MUCH MORE CREATIVE WHEN I'M DEPRIVED OF SLEEP LIKE I AM RIGHT NOW. BUT THIS MORNING THE IDEAS AREN'T FLOWING FROM ME LIKE THEY HAD BEFORE, THEY'RE NOT POURING FROM MY FINGERTIPS AS MY MUSE BANGS OUT A RHYTHM ON HIS MAGICAL BONGO DRUMS TO GENERATE AMBIENT WONDER AND AMAZEMENT THAT MATCHES MY PRESENT CRAZINESS.
I HAD AN HONEST VISION OF WHERE THIS WAS GOING BUT IM NOT FEELING IT RIGHT NOW—>IT SEEMS TO BE GOING NOWHERE AND NOW I M GIVING UP   MAYBE LATER, WHO KNOWS?

The wrong place at the wrong time is really the right place at the right time in disguise. Look under the fabric of dirt and grime and you'll find adventure. Things that are crass and gritty have more character than things that are plastic and pretty. I'd rather stand in a pile of shit than go to a famous nightclub with Paris Hilton; I'd rather rob a bank than win the lottery. I'd rather bomb a church than join one.

A Socially Constructed Prison

IT DRIVES ME CRAZY

This drives me crazy. I can't stand when people get a tiny glimpse of me and then think they understand me and my style. No, you haven't even begun to understand me and my style. Like, sometimes people will read a story or a poem by me and think they understand my style, so they throw me a harmless suggestion, like maybe you should practice writing in third-person more so you can get better at that. But I have stories in third-person too. Just because they've only seen one story by me that's in first-person does not mean all my stories are in first person. It drives me crazy. And vice verse: I show someone a story in third person and they tell me I should practice writing in first person more. Like, at the bar last night, this girl who'd seen me read only once was telling me there's a time and place for everything. But I know that. In fact, I know that very well. And every time I perform I try to read the crowd and asses what is best for me to read, I really do. But I can't read minds, and I'm not perfect, and at the one and only time she'd seen me read I happened to tank it, so she assumes I ALWAYS tank, she assumes I don't ever try to read the crowd. She assumes that that tiny glimpse of me says all there is to know. It drives me crazy when people do that.

my mind is like a labyrinth
complete with all sorts of twists and turns, all sorts of dips and rises that wind their way through layer after layer of madness

getting lost is just an unfortunate consequenc to having a rather complicated complex....

Leave behind your preconceived notions about who you want me to be, and bring a pen and a piece of paper if you wanna take notes, because boy are you in for a surprise.

29

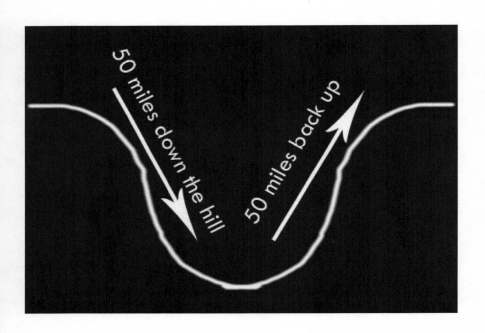

50 miles down the hill

50 miles back up

Oh, the sick thoughts that cross my mind when nobody's around.

If only you knew....

It's late in the night, and I feel I feel I feel like I'm waiting for something. But what>>>> It's late in the night and my mind races something fierce, speculating or whatever it is that my mind does late in the night. It's so late so late and the whole world sleeps. I think about things as the whole world sleeps. Sometimes I wonder about things, pondering deeply and spaciously until my pondering ceases and I fall asleep

It's late in the night and I hate I hate that there's nothing to do here. I sit up in my room and wonder why there's not a thing to do.   NOTHING at all

The nighttime has a mind too, a big mind fat mind, a mind that makes me feel oh so fine and alone and sometimes I like it but sometimes I don't,,,,,,,,,,,,,,,,,,,,,

The mind races while the body sleeps, my mind's hollow and my body feels steep, like a hill rising through hell and dropping to the depths of heaven.   So Alone.

Sometimes I hope for zzzombies==   for an epic apocalypse, for something that would make life better   and more interesting too: something I could do in this hole other than just doing myself like I did just yesterday and tonight, again and again until my skin blisters and bruises and I fall asleep with my dick in my hand.

I'm utterly bored, fairly alive, and in an epic wasted monotonous slumbr

I write, I do art.
I wait and I pace.
Anxiety can be a bitch
when you have nobody
to direct it at....

I wonder
pray to the sky
why nobody cares about
little old me, and the things
that I do.

I'm a terminal
social suicide, making new friends
and losing them constantly.
I'm destined to be no one
destined to nothing
nowhere and it's no fun.

Why me is my anthem.
I thought one day I'd
get over this feeling, the feeling of
hopelessness.

THE FEELING THAT
every attempt is futile
and therefore why should I care.

I don't know.
You tell me.
Help me see the light.
Help me get through this
emptiness I'm losing myself to.

I'm lost in a rut   a rut, and
it sucks. I want out now.
Let me out of this world.
Take me on your space shuttle
next time you're in town.
Fly me around the moon so that
for once I can feel good and alive
and for once I wont haveta cry.

AND I CRY....

Well, not really; I don't exactly know how.

STILL YOUNG

SOME THINGS JUST NEVER CHANGE

In **RUTland**
people are so 2-faced
 and I think I know why.

A smile around here
feels like a knife to the back,
 and I think I know why.

It's a survival technique
 I learned from living around here for quite
 some time

Be nice or die
 you'll get eaten alive by all the close-minded
 folk who live in these parts

It's funny, in
BOstOn, all the time
I'll meet someone and
then never see them
again. In Rutland,
that never happens.
YOu meet someone and
then start seeing
them EVERYwhere.

36

This means the country is in distress.
The upside-down American flag means
this country is in distress.

This country IS in distress
isn't it?
I do not hate America.
I do not hate
this country. BUT
I do believe this country is
going down the tubes.
don't you?

Insightful Segment from
Chaos Writing:

An Art Exhibit

I told them how the Chaffee Art Center in Rutland is so generic, so commercial, and I got a room full of nods. One woman piped in saying, But not in Stowe! No, it's not like that in Stowe.

I wanted to say, Everyone likes to believe their art is not generic, because it's their art, it's their children, and no one likes to think of their children as regular, as boring, they like to think of their children as special and interesting, because it's their children, they raised them....

But this is not always the case

Although I kept my mouth shut on that point. Realized I didn't need to point out the fallacy with, "But not in Stowe!"

Don't hate me for the words I use.

Hate me for the things I do.

GET THAT STRAIGHT!!!

I'm psyched	1	2 3
run wild	Help	run free
mania		

40

sometimes i dream of things. big things, sometimes small, but mostly big & unobtainable, out of reach for the likes of me. i guess i dont dream as much as i used to, now that i think about it. (when i say dream, i mean fantasy, by the way.) i cant remember the last real dream (fantasy) i had—cant remember what it was about. maybe that means ive lowered my expectations some. i mean, i used to be a bit of an idealist, always in an existential (dressed-up nihilism) funk. it really got me down. you see, i claimed to be a nihilist—only i always pronounced the word wrong even tho i knew the actual pronunciation (i dont believe in pronouncing words properly, id say—pure nihilism—because id grown up pronouncing it this way (niy-ilism) my whole life & i wasnt gonna change for nobody)—but i cud never accept that there was nothing beyond the scope of vision. there is nothing, i know now, or maybe theres something, i dont know—either way the answers i seek are too dense for my finite brain to comprehend, so i jus leave it like that: it is what it is, it was what it was, the past is carved in stone, cant be changed by anyone, especially not by me, & the future is a mystery waiting to be revealed. if only i had foresight, cud somehow see the future. if i had super powers. or even if i jus had access to money that cud afford all that i need & then some & then maybe i cud buy my girl a nice leather jacket for halloween. she'd put it on, id wrap my arms around her, & instantly we'd float up up up & up, straight up until we're airborne, flying thru the dark, cloudy sky like two super heroes in luv. see what i mean? & then id work myself into a fit when reality snaps back in & id crack my chin on the stone cold existence that is my life: a baby brought into this world for gods sick enjoyment—wait, i thought we established that there is no god; either way there might be some form of deity in the clouds watching over us, & the day—morning, afternoon, or evening; one or the other—i weaseled my way outta my mothers womb & took my first whiff of pure air, the deity, eyes insanely wide, jaw suddenly dropping, tongue hanging loose & sloppily in its shapeless maw, a rumble growing in its gut, stirring fierce & frightening, surging up into its chest, past where its heart wud be if only it were human, up thru its throat, & exploding from its mouth in cackling hysteria, died of laughter—the deity died that day, god is dead, faith is dead, & i fuckin killed it & now ive gotta live w/ that, w/ all the knowledge that i damned the human race to hell, if such a thing even exists in the first place. i mean, dont get me wrong, im not exactly anybody special or anything; im jus another bozo on the bus, as they say, along for the ride. really, that whole bit about me killing god is jus another one of my dreams—or moreover, nightmares. like i said, i havent had a legitimate dream in years; but this godforsaken brain of mine, it doesnt ever stop. its like an endless film reel spurning out a travesty of situations that i can easily project into the real world, & sometimes, if not most of the time, these projections really get me down, so i try not to think about it. i let the nightmares churn deep in my subconscious & i dont try to fight it, because when i jus let it happen & maybe laugh about it later, these torturous images dont seem to carry as much weight & i can easily brush them away w/ a simple flick of my wrist. they come & go & i dont know, i guess ive come to luv my lack of dreams & my knack for horribly visceral nightmares that pray on me when im asleep at night. i wudnt trade them for anything. because after all, dreams make me feel worse. wake up from a wonderful dream & where are you? how do you feel now? now that your fantasy has faded away & reality sets in harder than ever like a haymaker punch straight to your face. but wake up from a terrible nightmare, & boy, am i so glad to be back home....

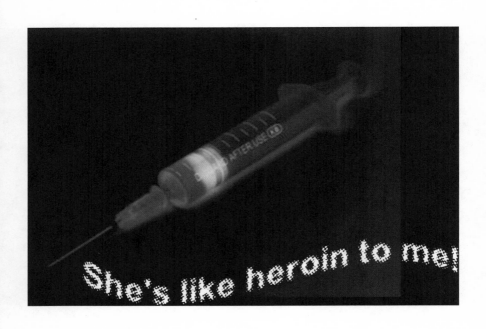

jam the round peg into the square hole,
and jam it hard,
make it fit,
lube it up;
do everything possible to get in.
it's important that we succeed
in making the thing fit.
it's vital that we bash it till it sets.

bang it up,
bash it in,
and keep on smashing that peg.

dings are denting the sides.
cuts and crevices break out like hives.
the peg is starting to look misshapen;
starting to lose its shape.

that only means we've gotta
bash it in harder.

My head hurts
aches
is falling apart

My brain melts
stings
is turning to ashes

My mind bleeds

Living
FASTER

Playing
LOUDER

1-2-3-4

opened-wide
a slapdash of random thoughts
are racking my insides
smacking my outsides
and I run & hide!

Fuck
rock & roll
I can't
dance
I'm a bad
driver
I like to
jerk off,
don't you?
Fuck
rock & roll

you just dont get it, Mr. MAN. you dont get why i need my music fast, why i seek loud, out-of-sync noise, why the beats are smashing, the riffs are thrashing, and the vocals are glass-shattering——no, you do not understand why; but i can assure you there is a method to my madness, a reason I thrive for loud, fast music....

it mends the wounds in my head, it mends the scars crisscrossing my brain, and it mends the madness bleating inside my mind.

so   there!

44

I mean I'm a drunk and a pill-popper, addicted to more and more and more, and I live—no, I thrive for excess; I chase the Pink Dragon like it's my occupation. From one hurdle to the next, I rise higher and grow stronger, and when the Pink Dragon seems to be getting closer to me, it's farther than ever, and I keep after it, picking up speed, swirling my lasso, and hurling it but it always lands just an inch to the left or the right, but that's okay, because one of these days I'll catch it and choke it and then I'll feel whole and alive, like I had reached my goals, but my goals are always too far out of reach. . . .

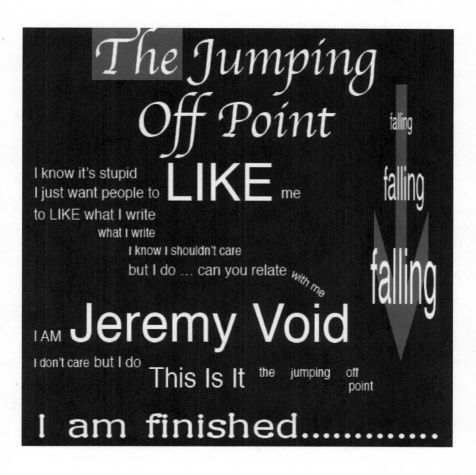

I'm trying to fit	learning to lie	I wanna be //
I wanna be them	but every single time	
		I get knocked back a peg....

48

the Sick & the Twisted

it's not that i'm a negative person, because i'm definitely not, although i do have my times; it's just that i enjoy the Sick & the Twisted.

i want to delve into it.
i want to explore it.
       fuck it
       torture it
i want to scalp it
rip out its brains
put it on display
       under the microscope

and watch as all those tiny little atoms that make up the realm of the absolutely FUCKED UP fight and fuck and kill eachother with battleaxes and tommy guns and switchblades and their own fuckin teeth and nails—

(WORLD WAR XXX)

49

I WANNA START AN ART REVOLUTION! WHO'S WITH ME????

I found out yesterday that the Chaffee
Art Center screens what art they allow in
Art in the Park. No wonder all the shit
they sell there is so lame.

THE STORY OF MY LIFE

I Told This Girl That I Was Crazy
She Didn t Believe Me
She Got Too Close
and now she hates me

Say you dress in counterculture clothing, such as sporting large spikes on your leather biker jacket and a torn T-shirt that you tossed in the path of a lawnmower while working landscaping one day because you were curious about what the outcome might be, like what kind of design would develop in the damage, and through the wreckage people can see your messy tattoos that were done with a safety pin in someone's crummy basement. Your hair, too, is messy, with clumps of soap that look like cum stuck to the strands, and your eyes are blood-red. On closer inspection one can see the red veins zigzagging like streaks of lightning from the outer rim of your eyeball to your blue pupils that are so bright they actually accentuate the redness. But that's not why you see red. No, it's not. You see red because you and two friends were forced against a wall by the police for no other reason than the way you were dressed—and because a kid played basketball with your head one night outside of Store 24; he dribbled your skull on the cold concrete, making murderous threats. He would have killed you if it weren't for the cab driver who saw it all happen. Of course, those are not the only reasons you see red. Those are only two examples from your life. I mean, you can't forget the time your cool older brother invited you to hang out with his friends because your own friends … *what friends?* … and in one of his friend's front yard you took a terrible beating from the bastards while the kid's dad just watched it go on, thinking, you assume, that boys will be boys and that it's not a big deal, they're only roughhousing, playing around. To you it sure didn't feel like a game. *YOU WERE ONLY A LITTLE KID!!!* Or do you remember the time you were on the swings while your sister swung on the swing next door, and she dropped her McDonald's toy? Do you remember the two kids who took it off the ground, and when you asked for it back, the taller of the two launched his fist into your gut and you fell to the ground crying? You were in so much pain. That was before the rebellion developed deep in your heart. The anger and frustration you feel first showed itself when you were in ninth grade attempting to fit in, and you wore all the right clothing and walked and talked just like them, but your sad attempts at acceptance only gave you a blackened eye and a swollen lip. So you gave up, and your infamous streak of disorder started from there, and the beatings from bullies and cops continued, only today you are true to yourself and you at least fight back, having developed in your heart a sense of dignity.

Insightful Segment from
Chaos Writing:

Irrelevant Battles

I don't really give a shit how far you're able to piss. And I'm certainly
not going to try my hand at pissing any farther.   It's just not
worth my time.

That kind of battle is so irrelevant.
I've got more important wars to fight, more important battles to pick.
My friend is currently detoxing from heroin, and I'm giving him a hand,
giving him a chance at a better life.

So,   sometimes it's just not worth it.
          Don't try and convince a catholic that there is no god;
          don't attempt to tell an atheist that there is.

How the hell
can they be so sure?
anyway

faster/slower

faster faster faster
thats what theyd say
when their life zips thru existence
like a laser beam.

slower slower slower
thats what theyd say
when theyre walking thru a minefield
that their fast-paced life had led them to
in the first place.

i know nothing   i know nothing   i know nothing   i know nothing

What You Believe & The Principles You Practice are not my business to try and change

ya dig!

i know nothing   i know nothing   i know nothing   i know nothing

sometimes

sometimes i act real crazy
but i can assure you my heart
is always there, it always beats
& throbs as i pass thru the
bloody rainbow into your mind.

sometimes i want to unwind,
but i cant find it, the answer is blind.
sometimes my mind races.
it races & i get restless & pace.

my brain beats like a heart,
pumping knowledge into me like
im receiving a reverse lobotomy.
i dont know why that happens why its
the case except that it happens
& my brain melts into ashes.

i know you think that im weird.
did i tell you i can read your mind?
i know you think that im strange.
did i tell you that i am in fact
deranged .... so much its like
im my own mother & father having
conceived me when i was a toddler.

i sometimes live as fast as
a runaway freight train robbed by
gangster cowboys w/ hatchets.
other times my life moves like a
snail squirming along as it
wins the race. those times
when im the slowest are the times
when i feel the farthest left behind.
i feel like ive gotta catch up
because if i dont the world
will explode & itll all be
my fault.

i wudnt be able to live
w/ myself in the absence of
reality the real world everything
youve come to know & luv but
which ive come to know & despise.
all of that crap i know now is so utterly
important & yet i wish for it to
be nuked like apple pie. be eaten
like a chimpanzee eats maggots off
the dead flesh of a fallen beast
in the wild west & you know
exactly what im saying only
im sure you really dont.

youre as lost as i am
probly so now ive gotta cry....

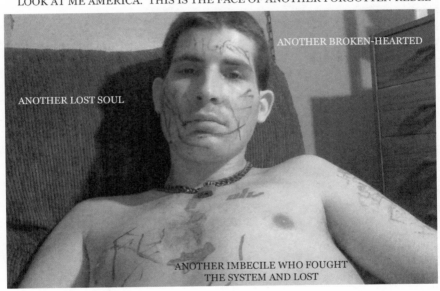

LOOK AT ME AMERICA. THIS IS THE FACE OF ANOTHER FORGOTTEN REBEL

ANOTHER BROKEN-HEARTED

ANOTHER LOST SOUL

ANOTHER IMBECILE WHO FOUGHT
THE SYSTEM AND LOST

While you're off living your Hallmark lives....

IN MY WRITING I SAY THAT I DON'T CARE ALL THE TIME, BUT THE TRUTH IS, I CARE WAY TOO MUCH—WAY, WAY TOO MUCH. I DON'T WANT TO CARE, THAT'S TRUE. I WISH I DIDN'T CARE, THAT'S TRUE. I PREACH NOT CARING, THAT'S TRUE.

BUT—AND HERE'S THE BIGGIE—I KNOW WE SHOULD NOT CARE ABOUT WHAT OTHERS THINK, BUT THAT DOESN'T MEAN THAT I DON'T.

I MEAN, I'M ONLY HUMAN!

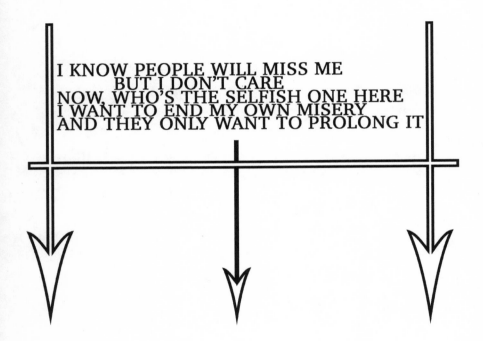

I KNOW PEOPLE WILL MISS ME
   BUT I DON'T CARE
NOW, WHO'S THE SELFISH ONE HERE
I WANT TO END MY OWN MISERY
AND THEY ONLY WANT TO PROLONG IT

OH NO I HOLD ON FOR
MY DEAR LIFE BUT THE BOAT IT
ROCKS & THE EARTH IT TURNS.
THE CARS RUNS A RED LIGHT
SPEEDING OUTTA CONTROL.

STOP STOP STOP. TAP TAP TAP
THE MAN IS SPEAKING MY EYES
ARE TWEAKING
AS I SEARCH THE STREETS FOR SOME
SPEED SPEED SPEED.

CHANGE CHANGE CHANGE
WE'RE CONSTANTLY CHANGING
& I FUCKIN HATE CHANGE.
WHERES THE RESET BUTTON,
RESTART IVE MADE A MISTAKE
I WANNA DO IT AGAIN I WANNA START
FROM SQUARE ONE & DO IT
ONE MORE TIME J US ONE MORE TIME.

BUT
IT
WONT
EVER
STOP.

MY HEARTBEAT QUICKENS.
MY PULSE SPIKES.
THE BABY GROWS OLDER
& I FEEL LIKE A TODDLER
WHERED THE TIME GO .

CHANGE CHANGE CHANGE
THE WORLD IS CHURNING & ONE DAY
THE SUN WILL EXPLODE.
BUT NOT IN MY LIFETIME THEY SAY BECAUSE
ILL BE DEAD & GONE BEFORE THE WORLD
ENDS BEFORE IT BURNS DOWN BEFORE
THE ZOMBIES RIZE UP FROM THE GROUND
AN APOCALYPSE IS
AMONG US & ITS CHANGING
BUT I FUCKIN HATE CHANGE.
CHANGE CHANGE CHANGE

WHY WONT IT STOP

Mr. Media
Mrs. Mainstream
the most devious marriage
they're always popping out offspring
of yesterday's rebellion
who grow up to be today's trend.
It happened to black people
it happened to Punks.
What culture will they vomit on next?
One day they're fighting against
the next day they're fighting with
and then they forget the fight
and instead are fucking right
making more babies
who will grow up and rape
another counterculture.
That's the state we live in.
Goodbye badboy
hello radboy!
Hello mainstream rebellion
who reap Rules & Restrictions
and create just one more fad
to make me wanna kill myself to///
It's just so so so sad that

I don't fucking know anymore.

~~Communicated~~

You've Been

SACKED

YOU CAN'T PLEASE EVERYONE. SOMETIMES YOU CAN'T PLEASE ANYONE. BUT IF YOU'RE LUCKY YOU MIGHT PLEASE SOMEONE. BUT IN ANY CASE THEY REALLY SECRETLY HATE YOU AND THERE'S NO POINT IN TRYING ANYWAY CUZ THEY'LL NEVER SEE IT YOUR WAY.

SOO SIIIIICK TODAY

Warped

YOU PERCEIVE ME ONE WAY

but you don't see my inner torment

but you don't see the sick thoughts in my head

What the fuck are you looking at?

but you don't know me like I do

but you only see my carefully crafted reflection

BUT LET ME TAKE off this MAKEUP for JUST A MiNUUtE

You don't see what I see when I'm looking in the mirror

aaaaahh!!!

but the mirror is CRACKED

I DON T WANT TO BE REJECTED
I DON T WANT TO BE DENIED
I DON T WANT TO BE HERE AND
I DON T WANT TO BE THERE

I DON T WANNA LIVE IN
A WORLD WHERE I CAN T BE ME
PEOPLE JUDGE BUT THEY DENY
THAT THEY DO
PEOPLE HATE BUT THEY ACT
LIKE THEY DON T

HYPOCRITES I M THE BIGGEST ONE
BUT THE THING IS I
DON T DENY IT AT ALL
I REFUSE TO
I REFUSE TO DO ANYTHING
OTHER THAN WHAT I M DOING
RIGHT NOW I DON T LIKE YOU

YOU RE FAKE BUT SO AM I
YOU RE TOO LATE AND I
M THE ONE WHO TAKES THE BLAME
I M RUNNING WITH THE CROWD
I M WORSHIPPING THEIR GODD
WEARING THEIR CLOTHES
AND TALKING IN THEIR DRAWL

AND NOW YOU WONDER WHY I HATE
MYSELF AND WANNA BASH IN
MY OWN FUCKING FACE YOU WONDER
WHY SUICIDE SEEMS LIKE A SOLUTION
CUZ I M NOT YOU AND I WOULD RATHER
DIE DIE DIE

DON T YOU SEE THIS SOCIETY
IS BLIND AND CAN T SEE NOTHING AT ALL
WE RE LOST TO THE TV AND THE MOVIES
AND MAGAZINES THAT MAKE YOU STUPIDER
THAN THE FOOLS WHO PREACH ABOUT GOD

I HATE YOU AND YOUR VIEWS
I DISAGREE WITH YOU AND
WHY YOU CHEAT AND LIE AND THROW
IT ALL AWAY I D RATHER DIE

sounds like the best idea I ve heard all day.

72

I HATE MEMES. Again, someone just called one of my pieces a fucking meme. I'll say it again: I HATE MEMES. These are not memes. Memes are silly graphics that make light of a stupid situation. I am an artist, and in my opinion, memes are the lowest form of art, they cater to the lowest form of human, they are stupid at stupid's best.

Wikipedia says a meme is " 'an idea, behavior, or style that spreads from person to person within a culture'. A meme acts as a unit for carrying cultural ideas, symbols, or practices that can be transmitted from one mind to another through writing, speech, gestures, rituals, or other imitable phenomena with a mimicked theme. Supporters of the concept regard memes as cultural analogues to genes in that they self-replicate, mutate, and respond to selective pressures."

Goddammit, I hate this culture and its stupid practices. I'm willing to bet that memes weren't even around before social media, which means back then what I did would be respected and appreciated as REAL art; not as silly analogues to promote silly ideas, but as REAL word art, as REAL visual poetry, as something for a smarter kind of human, the kind shunned and disrespected by the mass majority because the masses could never understand, comprehend, or relate.

Not that scholars would ever respect me anyway.

Ode to Facebook.

So many faces.

So many names.

So many places.

I can't keep it straight.

THINK! I've gotta write something. THINK! What's there left to say? I've said it all already, hashed it out on page after page after page, and now I'm stumped. THINK! I'm thinking but the ideas aren't coming to me as easily as they once were. THINK THINK! C'mon, I've gotta strain my brain; it's a muscle, right? so I've gotta drain it, filter out the wisdom from the nonsense. THINK! Maybe I'm not thinking hard enough cuz I can't come up with new ideas anymore. It's a losing battle: at war with the muse. It's like she left the building, went on strike until I took better care of her. THINK THINK THINK! For Godsake, THINK!!!

Chapter 1:
The image is dented

Chapter 2:
The image is cracked

Chapter 3:
The image falls apart

—On Mindfulness

Today is Thursday, and I'm sitting here in the now, overly mindful of tomorrow. How can I be alive if I spend all my time writing about life? Writing is like the opposite of mindfulness. How can I write about the moment, in the moment? It would be like: I touch the pen to the line, I move it along the line to write words and then sentences and then ... well ... that's writing about the moment because in the moment I am writing. So I write about yesterday's world, about all the adventures, the misadventures, and the fetes I never crossed; and I write about tomorrow's world, about my dreams and aspirations—or lack thereof. This is my life as a writer. When I'm not writing, I try to stay in the here and now, but when I am, I turn this mindfulness on its side, kick it in the head, and claw out its eyes. Yesterday tomorrow left right up down, but never dead-center in the here and now. That's just how life goes ... for me! 24 hours a day, 224 words a page, give or take.

I'm sitting in my library I'm
listening to the Saints I'm
planning on going to the
open-mike tonight at Pub 42
I'm bored out of my skull I'm
waiting for something or
another but I don't know
what stop looking at me I
wonder I ponder I hate hate
hate that's all I've got to say
right now see you later when
the world dissolves in battery
acid
fun times
right?

RIGHT!

Kick em in the eyes
and claw out their balls

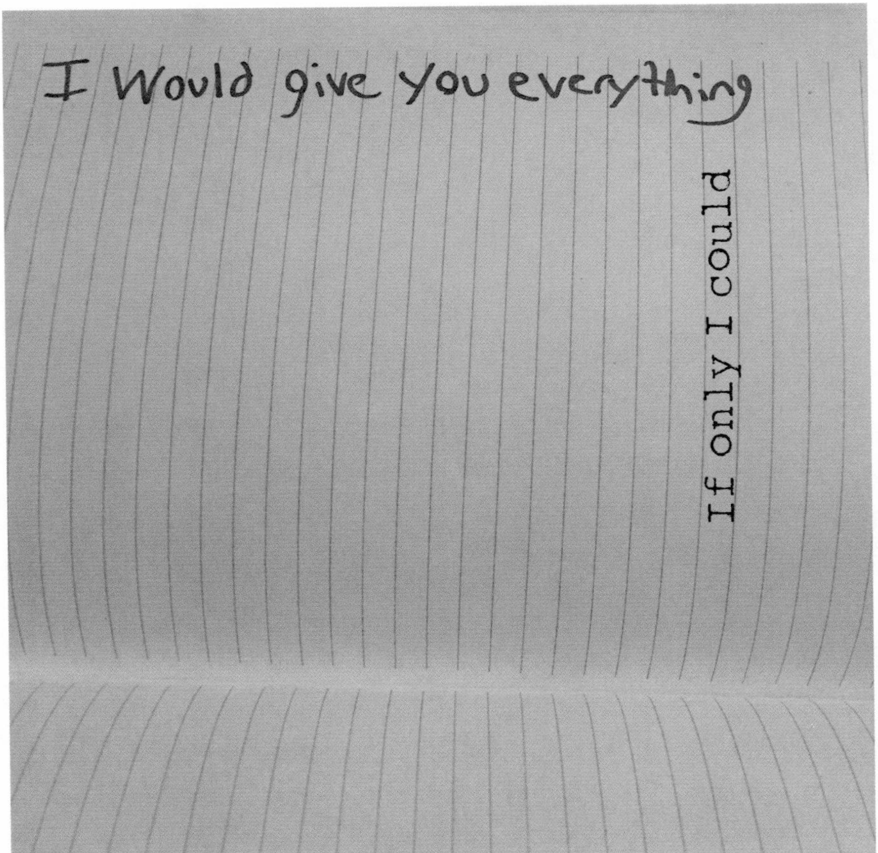

I Would give you everything

If only I could

Most people avoid dark places
        I don't.
It's like they're afraid of
what they'll see
what they'll find
who they'll be
when they come out the other side

        Me, I embrace the dark.
        I welcome dark forces with
                open arms
        If you look close enough into
        dark places
        you'll find the truth
        glimmering like a ghoulish rumination
        so bright and vivacious
        it makes me feel alive
        like I'll never
            be the same
                again . . . .

the music plays fast
i got a headache
            I Want It Faster
or the pain in my head
will never settle. . . .
            PLAY IT LOUDER

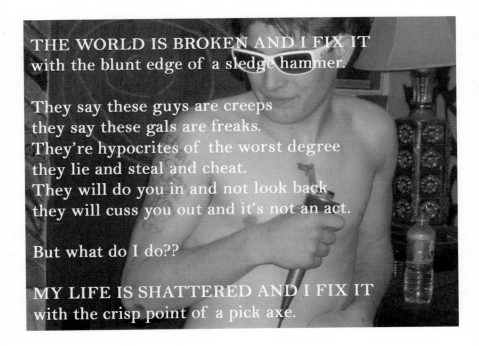

THE WORLD IS BROKEN AND I FIX IT
with the blunt edge of a sledge hammer.

They say these guys are creeps
they say these gals are freaks.
They're hypocrites of the worst degree
they lie and steal and cheat.
They will do you in and not look back
they will cuss you out and it's not an act.

But what do I do??

MY LIFE IS SHATTERED AND I FIX IT
with the crisp point of a pick axe.

If I had a gun, I'd probably put it in my mouth and blow my brains out. I don't know why I even bother trying in the first place. I've had a really fucking rough upbringing, what with me not fitting in and just getting shit from my peers all the time, and now I'm older and you'd think life would get better or at least even out, because everyone has their day, as they say; but then where's my day? I'm still a social cretin, and things don't get better, they only stay the same or get worst, is what I've always believed my whole life. But then I abandoned that prior notion when I started attending AA cuz I saw other people getting better—but that's great for them. Because for me things either stay the same or get worst, and if I had a gun I'd put it in my mouth and blow my brains out right now.

A Story About Nothing

This is a story about nothing—it's absurd and pointless; you might not get it at first or ever, but you know what, I don't really care because nothing matters anymore.

This is a story about nothing—I lived it and I loved it and I come to realize that the life I lived swallowed me up, yum yum yum, and spit me out. I learned that the hard way, I never came to until I came to Vermont, living in a daze, every single day, a haze, everything fading away.

This is a story about nothing—just remember, kids, try it and see what happens. You could die. Just remember, kids, don't live like I did. It's no way to exist.

This is a story about nothing—the end.

But nothing really speaks to me, nothing really stands above anything else. Everything is nothing, nothing is everything; love is hate, hate is love, it's all the same to me in the end. It's life, it's sex, it's wonderful, it's terrible, I only have nightmares, but some of my nightmares make me wet, if you know what I mean. Although what is a nightmare if you're not crawling through vomit on your knees while demons in loin cloths whip you with spiked cement blocks that coil like a slinky and you're on your knees bleeding and you're screaming although you have a raging erection and it's spewing acid and you're wondering, How the hell did I end up in this predicament? It's one of those things where you know nothing will ever be the same again.

to-
day
was
bor-
ing

My day **started** slow, and then as time **progressed**, the pace **sped up** and soon I couldn't **take** it, I couldn't **take** it, I was **running** to **catch up** it **sped** right past me so quickly, and now it's the evening and I'm **sitting** here **wondering** where did it all go?

no-
thing
ex-
citing
hap-
pened
today

Wed., 11/21/2012
——6:27 PM

I have a hard time around family because I lack skills in acting formal or proper. When I used to live in Boston, before I moved to Vermont, I never learned the art of acting proper, as I seldom needed to act proper. I feel so ill-fit that I just isolate myself. I try to communicate like a "normal" person, but then I just get bored. I hung out with Bell last night and had a fun, sober time. For the first time in a very long time, I could be me, and it's so rare that I even socialize with people in the first place. Sitting or standing around talking proper bores me. That's why when I went to Stowe, VT, for Nana's birthday and to see family, Levi brilliantly suggested I talk about my writing, promote my stories, in fact bring a story to show around—I ended up bringing "The Haunted Bathroom." But I just feel so awkward, so out of place, like a stranger in a strange land. There are not too many people in Vermont who think and act like me, either, and even the other Punk rockers around here bore me too. The people who know me, such as other Spring Lake Ranchers, have learned to tolerate me because they've come to find out that I'm not such a dick after all, but rather, just very uncouth. So they let me be me—to an extent, of course—as long as I tone down my crass behavior, which I do—reluctantly. They let me be me as long as I respect their rights to feel safe. That's why I love Samantha so much: I can be me with her—more than anyone else. I can be uncouth with Bell and Andew and Alex, but not entirely me. It's 6:42. I'll probably leave in fifteen minutes. I wonder why Samantha hasn't called yet.

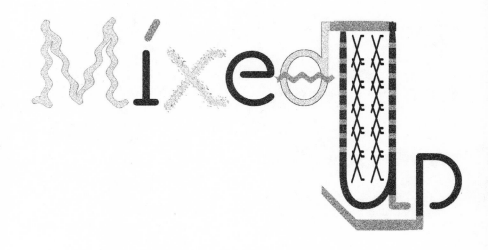

IT ISN'T OVER   IT ISN'T OVER   IT ISN'T OVER

keep it clean

my life, my rules

my life, my rules

my life, my rules

I don't take drugs...
beat people up who
try to beat me up

I don't have sex...
beat people up who   do I even wanna?
try to beat me up

I don't pick fights...
do I even care?

MINOR THREAT *said they're*
out   of   step

92

It would be a lot easier to be myself if I was a likable person, not so detestable, but a bit more sociable, well-versed in manors and social conduct and easy to get along with.   But no, I'm a repulsive little rat fink who lurks in the shadows and watches as you get your throat cut by that psychopath who lives around the block, you know the one.   I'm sneaky and conniving, a cretin a ghoul a kid with no class who only wants someone to understand him but I cannot achieve social bonding if I only be myself.   I'm no good, a social failure, and I know rejection like I know my own little big toe.   But anyway, your society is a joke.

PUNISH OR BE DAMNED

You work with a bunch of crazies
expecting everyone to act like a fuckin saint
Not gonna happen!

You work with a bunch of crazies
and get upset when someone acts a little erratic
What do you think is gonna happen????

round round round GAMES round round round round round round & & & & & & & & & &

I'm 28-years old

My moods are always in flux

I have no plans for the future

I have yet to find a place of belonging

I hate authority

I constantly abuse my mind and body

I'm 28-years old

and I just don't know what I want

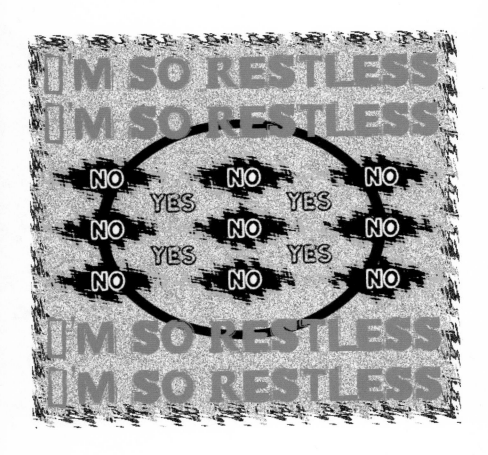

I think the point of life is to create. To learn and to create. We start out as babies knowing nothing about what's to come. We have no manuals about how to live our lives, either. We literally start from scratch, with nothing and without a clue. And then we get older and we learn and adapt to our surroundings. That's how the human race started, technology-wise, with nothing, but as life went on, we as human beings learned more and thus created more, and then dynasties were formed, destroyed, and formed again. It's in our nature, engrained in our DNA.

My skin bubbles delightfully beneath the array of colors coming together in the darkening sky, the soft mix of pale pink, orange, and amber magically touching my insides as I stare through the crisp evening sky. It's wonderful the way they form and glow and dance before my very eyes. I marvel, I stare, I watch, I behold the ever-changing, translucent sea of sparkling tones as they stream like confetti across the screen; they jump and dash, erratic splashes of decadent godliness painted across the blackening beyond.

Writing, for me, is like vomiting, only everything slows down and I can see the vomit coming out at a snail's pace and before it hits the page I clean it up and dress it nicely so that instead of vomit, ART HITS THE PAGE.

I get the last seat on the bus. I almost miss it too. I mosey up the steps and make my way down the aisle, then curse beneath my breath as I reach the end and turn around, thinking, This is just my—— But look at that. The elderly woman seven rows down from me swipes her bulky, sparkly black purse from the empty seat beside her. I shoot my glance to the front of the bus so as to calculate my chances of acquiring that seat before the young girl with pink pig-tails and a baby-blue bouse—maybe ten to twelve-years old—just bouncing up the steps, gently reaching into her pocket to remove her bus fair, counting it out in her hand slowly and with great care—one nickel … two nickels … three nickels (all the while the bus driver, I notice through the corner of my glare, is impatiently tapping the coin reader) … four nickels … five nickels…. When she counts out fifty cents (10 nickels), she begins dropping them in the slot—one nickel, clink; two nickels, clink; three nickels, clink; etcetera etcetera. She finally drops the last nickel in the slot, the bus driver sighs with great relief and cranks the lever to shut the door; she maneuvers her glare to point down the aisle of the bus proper—and then our eyes meet. We stay like that for a few beats, eye to eye, like an old-fashioned Mexican standoff, the bus veering out of its spot and cruising toward the exit of the lot, until the young girl winks at me—I swear, she actually winks, her right eye clamping shut and then barging open—and as if on cue I bolt for that seat, the last seat on the bus, right beside an elderly woman who doesn't want me sitting beside her, anyway. I run straight down the center of the aisle, knocking away purses and book bags that hang loosely in my path.

Just in the nick of time, I reach the seat and slip into it quickly, sliding right past the young girl who almost made it here first. I plop my butt into the rough, torn upholstery, risk a glance at the old woman sitting beside me, looking at me, glaring down through the eyes in her nose, a grimace that looks almost permanently placed distorting her ever so wrinkly face; and then look at the young girl standing in the aisle, tiny hands clutching her tiny waist, and she stares back, harder than any stare I could ever produce, her nostrils flared, eyebrows slanted, her chest heaving; she stares straight through me, takes in a deep breath, and snorts, "That wasn't very nice, *Mister*"—with snotty emphasis on the mister. Right after she says it, the most guilt I'd ever felt in my whole life at one time (times infinity) floods into me, pooling in my heart and festering in my brain. So with that I ease myself standing and slip into the aisle swiftly, but with an unsure air to my movements as she replaces me and drops into the seat and crosses her arms in one single, fluid motion, landing butt-first on the upholstery with a heavy, irritated *humph.*

A flower dipped in toxic waste
is a beautiful thing,
because the beauty of it
comes from the lack of knowledge
of what it will become.

A flower that grows straight
and maybe tips one way or another
seems boring
to me.

A flower that's unpredictable
intrigues me
so much more.

Punk didn't die
It just grew up.

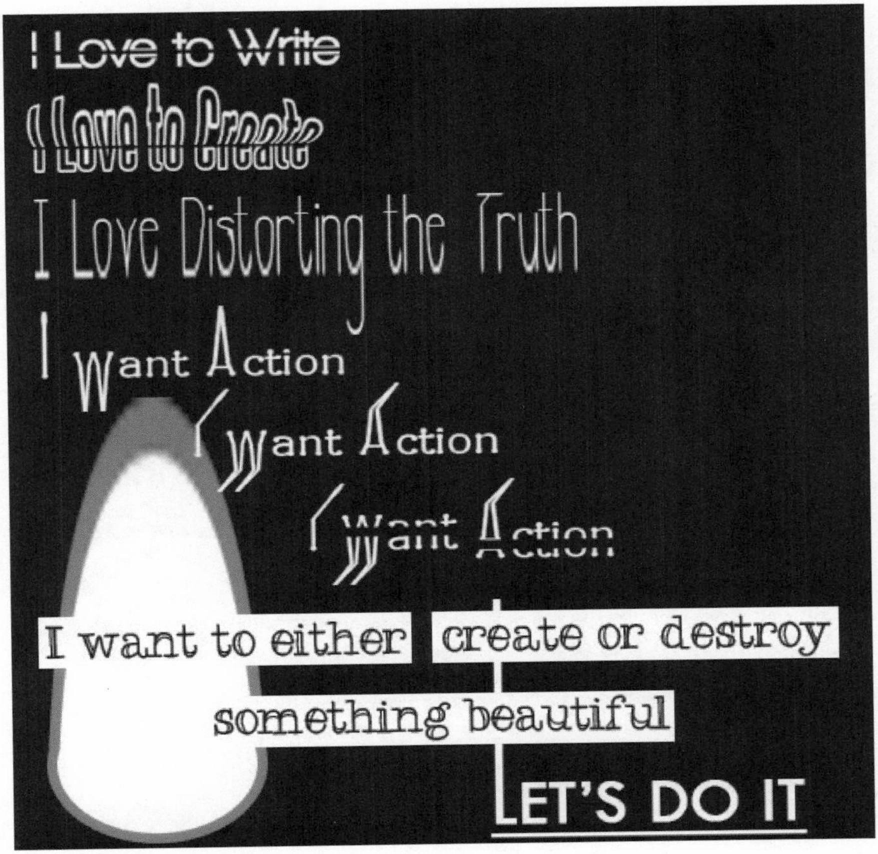

I Love to Write

I Love to Create

I Love Distorting the Truth

I Want Action

I Want Action

I Want Action

I want to either create or destroy

something beautiful

LET'S DO IT

I SING IN A DIFFERENT PITCH
I STRUM A DIFFERENT RIFF
I MOVE TO A DIFFERENT RHYTHM
& and that's right
I MARCH TO THE BEAT OF A DIFFERENT DRUM

THIS IS ME /// THAT IS YOU
I am perfect

Dancing Queen

Im not really a dancing guy
cuz the way I see it
if bones don't break
if noses don't fracture
if the floor isn't covered in
blood and guts by the end of the night
the only place you'll find me
        is in the corner snoring my face off

PEOPLE scare the fuckin shit out of me
She's more scared of me He Says
than I am of her.......

PEOPLE piss me off
to no end....
~~I run and hide~~,
but they find me there
ALWAYS

I feel cold.
I want you to warm me
in yours arms
hold me tight and tell me lies
about a better place
a place where even the misfits
fit in.

I need encouragement
Will you nourish me?
Pull me close and whisper dearly
about a world where even you and I
could be king, a world where the winners
lose and the losers thrive.

What do I gotta do to
get you to hold me?
What lies must I tell you
to get you to coddle me
to squeeze me in your arms
and tell me
it'll be alright.

Everything's gonna be fine.

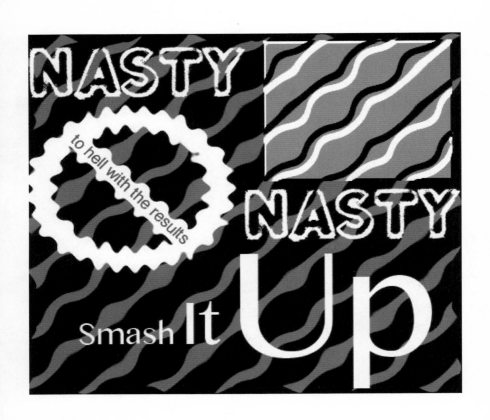

What You Need to Know

My goal isn't to bore you
It isn't to make you numb
You're dumb and that's your problem
My writing is not a drug.

It will not lift you up
It will not make you high
You might wanna die
But that's your problem, not mine.

"You must be using your mind in order to lose it"

Insightful Segment from
Chaos Writing:

Boston?

It's easier not to think about it. Out of sight, out of mind, as they say. But the future is coming too, as they say. But they also say the future is unwritten. Or at least that's what Joe Strummer said. For all I know staying in Rutland might be the most beneficial of the two decisions. Or if I went to Burlington, I might by chance meet Stephen King and he might by chance read one of my books—or all of them. I could go to California and get hit by a bus. I could go to New York and win the lottery. I could get on TV if I go to Texas.

There are cornfields in Kanas.

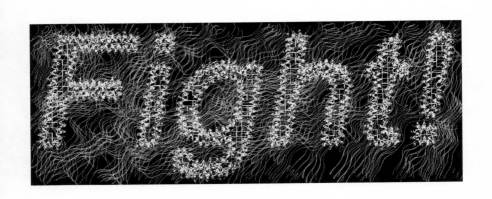

I NEED A FUCKING CIGARETTE. EVERY-
BODY FUCKING HATES ME AND I NEED
A FUCKING CIGARETTE. THE WORLD
HAS TURNED AGAINST ME AND I NEED
A FUCKING CIGARETTE. SOMEBODY
SHOOT ME DEAD BEFORE I SMOKE AN-
OTHER FUCKING CIGARETTE.

**Cuz I'd much rather die quick and painlessly than
live another day choking myself to death on tar and
rat poison.**

It's no way to fucking die.

Hate Your Neighbor

Revel in your
nastiness.
Celebrate your
hate.

If it keeps you occupied,
then who am I to say
you should not
feel this way.

Emotions are a
tricky subject,
a very tricky thing.
They give us
meaning, and they
show us the way.

They get us outta binds,
keep us from getting
stuck.
They keep us alive
and for that,
you can go and get
fucked.

We need a little
turmoil in
our miserable lives.
We need a little
controversy
to keep us alive.

Art is fueled by misery,
fueled by unhappiness alike.
Artists don't thrive on smiles,
nor do we live off of
kindness.

So I say:

Revel in your
nastiness.
Celebrate your
hate.

Do it for the sake of
everything that is
just a little bit irate.

We hate to live,
live to hate
and for that
we can all be

grateful.

it's not in my blood
it's not in my DNA

Why should I care
????????????????????????????????????

anyway

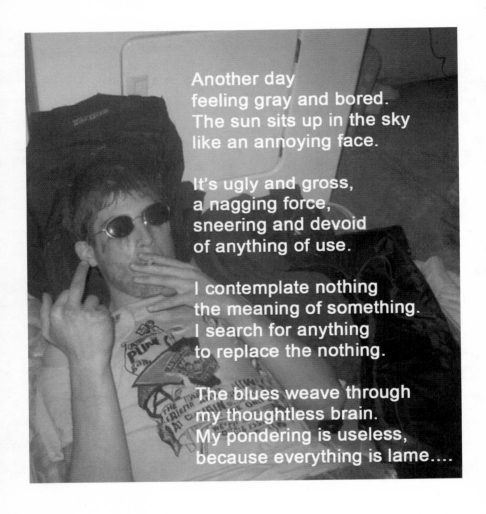

Another day
feeling gray and bored.
The sun sits up in the sky
like an annoying face.

It's ugly and gross,
a nagging force,
sneering and devoid
of anything of use.

I contemplate nothing
the meaning of something.
I search for anything
to replace the nothing.

The blues weave through
my thoughtless brain.
My pondering is useless,
because everything is lame....

Love is everything, Love is nothing…. Love will break you, Love will make you. One whiff of Love will lift up your spirits, until that whiff evaporates and you fall right off a cliff.

Love is manipulative, it speaks to you softly, chides you into following it into your own doom.

Love and mania go hand&hand, until those hands come apart, and before long you'll be spiraling down into a void of self-destruction.

Love soothes the mischievous, and Love eases the violent, but a loss of Love stirs them both into a roiling mass of turmoil.

We Love because it feels good—until that feeling loses its romance and sensation, and we fall to our knees and pray that we had never fallen in Love in the first place.

Love heals all wounds, brings fools together, spins them around in a cacophony of pleasure and catastrophic bliss, but just don't take away their Love … or the sky will come crashing down.

ive got nothing to say
but if i dont say something soon
i might jus dissolve
                disintegrate
                        evaporate. . . .

I am not having a very productive day.
The ideas are just not coming rushing
out of me like from an automated sprin-
kler. I'm losing steam, I'm sinking fast,
I'm crashing, I'm burning, the car runs
outta gas. There will be another day,
I'm sure, but today is all I see in the
here&now.

its cold outside
i stand in the road
i wait for something to change.

Suffering

I wanna get high,

but I don't.

I wanna have a life,

but I won't.

Living feels cold and depressing

and I want instant relief but

the only kind of relief I ever get

ties me up and beats me

with long bamboo sticks as trippy

midget demons prance around me in loin cloths

praising Jesus Christ ... and I'm scared.

No Offense, but

How many times have I been browsing down my Facebook newsfeed and I stumbled upon these great words (lyrics/poetry) and I comment THAT'S AWESOME DUDE. DID YOU WRITE THAT? and in response they go: NO, IT'S A SONG.

Like a slashed tire I then feel quite deflated because I liked those words, they were inspiring to me, but the perpetrator claimed they were only a quote.

Only A Quote.   A QUOTE!!!

Happens everytime....

Cra**ZY** right?

Last night I was explaining to this young guy that we should embrace insanity, welcome craziness into our lives with open arms, and later on, while sharing a cab with a younger couple, I started reflecting about what I was telling the guy earlier in the night about being crazy — Paranoid States of Consciousness — and I was thinking how mania isn't necessarily a bad thing, even though the system labels it as such, and the moment I started thinking about this, the guy I was sharing the cab with turned to his girlfriend and started talking about craziness and mania, like I was tapping into the collective conscious. I swear, in exact unison with my saying crazy in my own head, the guy said crazy out loud — in exact unison and rhythm with my own thoughts.

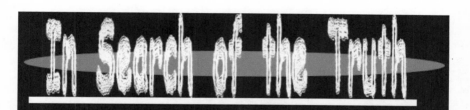

In Search of the Truth

The answers are escaping me.
These truths or so they claim
have got me wrapped up
in a blanket of lies.

All I want is the truth.
It's all I've ever wanted
all I've ever seeked
AND to get it I'll
do just about anything.

Steal cheat and lie
just to get by
just to get the answers
to see past your lies   lies that are

burning me up, beating me raw.
Lies that twist me inside out
and pelt me till I'm black and blue
with a long bamboo stick....

I'm sick and confused.
I'm startled and bemused.
I'm lost in a blundering hellhole
these lies swirling up past me
like a rising tornado tearing things apart
tearing me down
tearing out my eyes   cuz I don't
wanna see it anymore.

Why bother trying when
the whole world is a lie?
Why proceed when the people
        that I know
are only steering me wrong, pointing me to
a dead end and it's the only way
            to go....
The only way out of here

that I know.

If I wasn't so damn smart, I wouldn't think so intensely about everything, and as a result I wouldn't make such an ass of myself every chance I get. My voice might not quiver, like it does; I might speak louder and with more bronze to really project my voice so that the receiver isn't always having to say WHAT? after everything I say; I might even, like I used to do I think, act first and ask questions later, you know. But no, I've got this pestering voice lingering in the back of my mind telling me to halt. Just HALT!, don't do that, people will think you're foolish, they will be able to tell I've got borderline personality disorder, they will be able to read all the symptoms of my social anxiety, and yet NOBODY I'M TALKING TO HAS THE BRAINS TO DIAGNOSE ME WITH ANYTHING, let alone something as complex as BPD. These aren't trained individuals, these are commoners, people who bag my groceries, people who say WOULD YOU LIKE FRIES WITH THAT?. people who get brained senseless from watching relentless amounts of television, cuz you just never know what the Kardashians are going to do this week in stupid-ville. I've got nothing to worry about, of course. It's kind of like that stupid childish notion: if I can't see them, then they can't see me. Like, if I possess this knowledge, then EVERYone must possess it. You know, it really comes down to this: they KNOW. They know everything about me, and I can't get away from their judgmental stares, those judgmental cunts, so pedantic the way they stick their chins and their noses in the air and prance around like brain surgeons on their magic carpets of knowledge. FUCK, is all I can say. Fuck me and my obsessive obsessions, it's driving me mad!

Sorry about my rant here. Hope you can relate. Hope you pull the trigger before I do, cuz I'm sure to make a mess all over my bedroom wall. Fun, right? It's life 101, when you're smarter than the mass public, the slimeballs who think THEY'RE SMARTER THAN ME. Gimme a break. Peace!

Ha!

Ha!

Ha!

Life's not all fun and games!

Ha!

Says who?????

Ha!

Ha!

Why am I here?

Good question. I've been asking myself this a lot lately. There's the literal reason: because the birds and the bees got together and made nookey and nine months later the egg hatched and I somersaulted out of my mother's womb. Okay...and then what?! I was deformed and demented and this world had no place for me. The end.

But then there's the metaphysical reason, the abstract, and this gets more into philosophical reasoning. This is what my life had amounted to: For 28 odd years I surfed the seas of nothing, I squandered the void forest, I traipsed the plains of nowhere, and all for what? It's an endless cycle, this vicious spiral, plunging and twirling into nowhere.

I barely even exist....

Blankness

I've got n o t h i n g to say.
I'm drawing a blank—

My mind is slipping
and my eyes are too.
I'm losing consciousness
going to **sleeeep**
    soon....

They said I'm great for an adventure
They said I'm always off on these crazy adventures
taking mushrooms and getting all
tangled in barbed wire because I
couldn't find my way home
for 1

A Drug-&-Booze-Induced Existence

WAS MY LIFE

crazy

m
i
s
a
d
v
e
n
t
u
r
e

1 after another

another hit
another toke
another shot
another poke poke poke

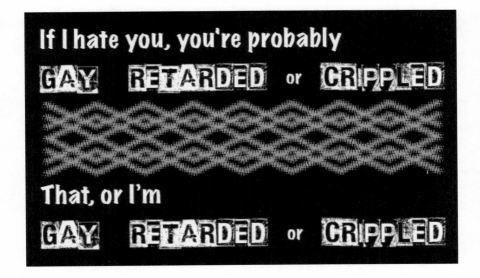

So blank,
like a piece of paper.
My body's numb
in a bathtub, of ice.
My thoughts,
they're depleted.
So bored,
I think I'll eat it.
The time is, I don't know.
I just don't care.
Death is a lumberjack
hacking at a tree trunk.

Karma's a real thing. You read "My Story: The Short Version," didn't you? In it, as you may or may not remember, some asshole forces himself on my girlfriend and I take the liberty of jamming a steak knife through the fat fucker's neck. Well, that asshole is dead now. Years later he was stabbed to death for forcing himself on the wrong dude's girlfriend. Karma's a real thing, I'm telling you; although it's not exactly the way the Buddhists say it is. Basically, you'll eventually piss off the wrong person, and I don't need to be the wrong person, cuz someone else will.

I FELT like there were no other options; & at the time I FELT like I was trapped, but I wasn't, I know now. I didn't have to resort to his level. I'm not sorry for the way I acted, & I do think it's hysterical that he got murdered in the same fashion I almost murdered him myself all those years ago, & I do think he deserved what he got for ruining other people's relationships like that, the scumbag he was. BUT there are always other options, I've learned in these past few years.

I wrote once, "Everyone is doing the best they can with the knowledge they think they know."

& I think that's a very powerful statement, it says a lot. When a person feels desperate, when they feel like they're trapped, they tend to act desperately. You can't expect anything more from a person in that state. But—mark my words—we are never trapped, this is AMERICA, and in America, we are never trapped. Just sometimes it feels like we are.

So remember that, next time you feel the need to act out just to prove that you are free!

Like I always say

If you can't create anything beautiful

Then Destroy

everything

beautiful

Hahahahahaha

shut the fuck
UP!!!

laminsane
fuckinggetusedtoit
goaway
ifyoucantacceptme
forwholam

Hey sweetheart cool off, you're not so distraught...
You lost what you had but that's what I've got.

No I'll close my eyes while you take off my clothes
wait a while till this feelings goes...

The feeling gets stronger, two times emptiness—
We'll embrace that much longer, make more of a mess...

Storm clouds roiling, a blast of lightning forks through. There's thunder, and it rumbles.
I nod my head and say,
Yes, ma'am.

I feel a wave of
kinetic energy intensifying,
my eyes seeing only red, a heat
in my forehead growing, the weight
of it all pressing down.

Walking on the street I imagine
I have powers that could
flip a bus on its side.
I stare at the cars that drive by,
pretending to blast them
with fireballs, knock them out
of orbit.

I wanna kill the passersby,
stab innocent bystanders
in their throats
and watch as blood pours from the holes
I have made.

I smile and say,
Thank you, ma'am.

Behind these eyes, dark clouds
spin tornadoes, they bring fire
and lightning and
acid rain.
I see rage, The Rage, and
it strengthens everyday.

A terrorizing wind to knock down houses and buildings and blow cars right off the road.

One day I will Snap!

The Rage

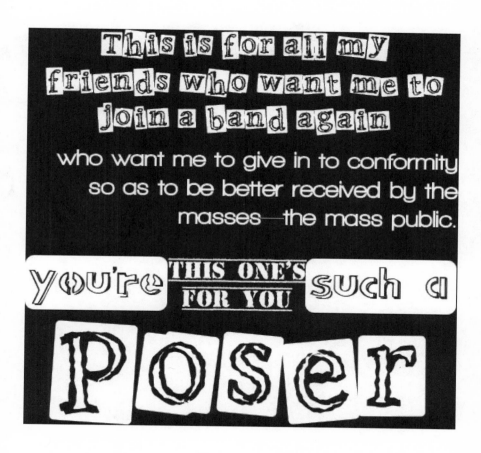

This is for all my friends who want me to join a band again who want me to give in to conformity so as to be better received by the masses—the mass public.

you're THIS ONE'S FOR YOU such a

Poser

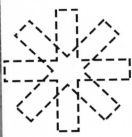

Disillusioned youth, won't you follow me.
We'll walk hand and hand into the flames.
We'll talk until the moon blows up
make plans to self-destruct.

The joke is broken, it's a caustic day.
The night is smoky, and we're young OK
Let's live for the system and tear it down
Let's die for rebellion and turn it around.

The world is ours and we feel so strong.
Our lives are theirs and we feel so dumb.
Let's go and creep through the streets of hell
We only need something to make us feel.

The land of the free, it's full of sissies.
The home of the brave, it's stuffed with rules
This is America, my friend, where they allow us rights
But they steal our rights so let's go and fight.

They steal our lives so let's go and die....

I'm a pretty boy with corrupted ideals.
My face is dirty but my thoughts are real.
What you see now is all you will see:
just a snot-nosed kid with rotting teeth.

I've dreamed of love, but dreams deceive.
All the love I'm giving you is all you'll receive.
I've got no remorse for shit I've done in the past.
If I've apologized to you, then I'm sorry 'bout that.

I'm not a poor kid and never was.
I can't fight and I'm not too tough.
But I'll say what I want and do as I say.
If you've got a problem with that, then come up to my face.

I've got dreams of ruling the whole human race.
I just wanna kill everyone who stands in my way.
Again, dreams deceive and hope is fake.
If you've got what I want, I will take.

I'm not a bad kid, but I'm not good.
I'm just a stupid kid who's been misunderstood.

Recovered Poem from 2011

I'm a user, a total loser
I'm a figment, a terminal delinquent
Can't exist without my fists
A demented twit, a little bitch
Can't decide on suicide
I been used & abused
Manipulated, so frustrated
& all this hatred is being wasted
You see me here without a tear
burning up inside, gonna let it loose on the outside
Hatred is all that makes sense to me
Broken bones are in my destiny
Throw a match into the gas
Fuck shit up & have a laugh
My jaded eyes have seen the way
The world's going to hell & I ain't afraid.

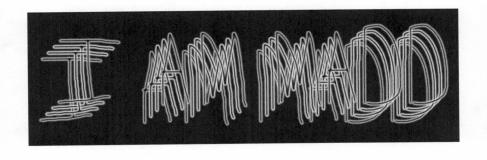

Hide

in the closet
& don't come out
until
the coast is clear.

If I were to speak for myself, I would say everything I've already said. I'm honest, I'm genuine, and although I do emulate from time to time, my voice, my thoughts, my ideas, are all my own. At one stage in my messy pubescence I admit my voice got watered down by peer pressure, I admit I lost my identity in an endless struggle to be cool.

But today my voice is my own. I'm a freak a loser and a cretin, but I'd rather be that than a victim of conformity. I'd rather be crazy than sane cuz to me sane represents repression. It represents bottled-up thoughts and ideas, feelings that are not permitted to see the light of day. I don't feel shame because shame is only a mere product of self-inflicted social etiquette.

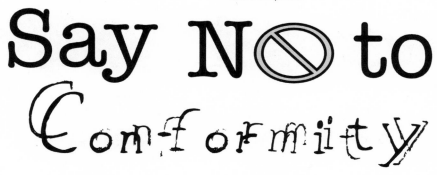

Say N⊘ to Comformity

Last night I met a guy named Scott. He said he used to work at Panera Bread with me. He knew my name already, he didn't have to ask. I knew his face, but I had to ask for his name.

My past is like a puzzle with all its pieces missing, and one by one the pieces are turning up so I can finally patch it all together, although I know it will never be over, not ever....

... to be continued....

Insightful Segment from
Chaos Writing:

Ugh

Ugh....
That's right——ugh....

Another day, another hour, another minute, another second, and I'm right
here right now typing about another nothing and what gives? It's all so
pointless—yadda yadda, blah blah blah, waiting again, and this patience
is killing me—blank and hopeless, running in a track of dismay cuz it's all
the fucking same....

So why do I do it?
Why not do it?
Why not do something else while I'm at it?
Another book, another chapter, another paragraph, another sentence, an-
other word to fill in this pointless rant about nothing and nowhere and it's
futile so much so why do I bother?

It's killing me—no royalties, no check in the mail; no fame, no recognition,
nobody even knows I exist ... what the fuck?

Would you believe me if I said I love you?
Would you hate me if I said I didn't?
Do you care enough to see the difference?
Or are you just dreaming that I'd leave you alone?

A cry for danger
A cry for madnes
A pleade for forgiveness
    All I see is ~~sadness~~

no regrets

A DEMON

A baby is born

t t t t
h h h h
e e e e
r r r r
e e e e is no

mommy
 mommy
  mommy
   mommy

is born

turning back

keep on fighting
keep on dying
your life is over
don't ever stop crying

I cried

153

PLAIN AND SIMPLE

I LIKE THE PRIVACY
OF MY OWN PERSONAL HELL.
I LIKE TO WRITE BECAUSE
I CAN DO IT ALONE.

I PLAYED MUSIC
PLAYED IN A BAND TOO,
BUT ALL THE STRESSES OF BEING
WITH OTHERS DROVE ME MAD

TO THE POINT OF....

I LIKE BEING ALONE.
I LIKE LIVING SIMPLY....
ALONE IS WHERE
I WANT TO BE.

PLAIN AND SIMPLE.

THE HEADLINES read
        another man
        dead
        another child
        abducted
        another young girl
        raped & beaten-
this i know-

i dont need the damn tv
to tell me this
the newspaper to spell it
out for me-

this i know. . . .

PERIOD

The world is in crisis
STOP
the terrorists have won
STOP
DRUGS & GUNS and prostitution
rule supreme and there's
no point in fighting it . . .
anymore
STOP STOP STOP

I've been told that
some people don't LIKE my posts
because they've got an image to uphold.

Well, I've got an image

to destroy!

Jeremy VOID

can't get out
can't get out
can't get out
can't get out
can't get out
can't get out

I look at the painting
on the wall
the EXIT sign glows,
reflected into my head.
I've come to the city
yesterday afternoon
just to sit
in an empty room
all by myself
thumbing through
my mental glossaries
        in search
        in desperate need of
        for I want
something
to satisfy
me—my desire to create
a world beyond
what I'm used to;
but there's no exit
from this surreal playground
and those four
glowing red
letters that spell out
EXIT
painted across the painting
bright and clear and beautiful
they mock me.
For I came
to the city
and now I'm sitting alone
in an empty room
as the dawn sprouts big hairy legs
and crests the mountainside
the time—five AM
the place—an empty room
in a crowded cabin
hidden deep in the depths of
an almost deserted wilderness.

No stars
no moon
no sounds
no movement
just me in an empty room
listening for the slight whisper
of the wind passing through
and the haunting murmur
the ominous gurgle
of sleeping bodies sleeping
but here I hear nothing
but my own steady breathing
and the cackle of flickering flames in the fireplace
and the crisp sound that my pen makes
as I form words on the page....

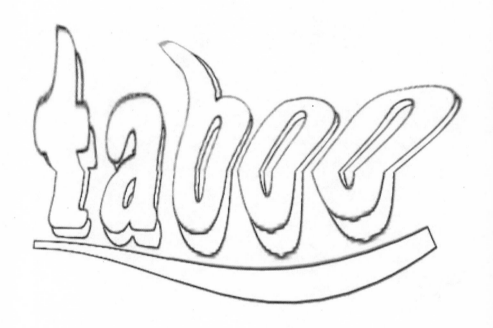

You wanna talk about vulgar?

Well, I hate to break it to you,

BUT

Censorship

is

VULGAR

(Actually
I'd be almost obliged to break it
to you.)

Insightful Segment from
Chaos Writing:

A Sex Inventory

On another note, there's one thing I don't understand about sexual conduct, and never have. Okay, they always say guys take advantage of girls, that they use girls for their own selfish purposes. I understand treating someone like a doormat or using them like toilet paper is wrong, but if the girl wants to have sex, is it really wrong to give her what she wants? Why is the guy always to blame in these situations? It's like, people complain that porn objectifies women, but what about the male porn stars? They're not being objectified? And they get paid less, too.

In our society, in our culture, it is always the guy taking advantage of the girl. And when I look back on it, I have taken advantage of some girls, but for the most part, they took advantage of me, and I only gave them what they wanted————is that so wrong?

You're not having a midlife crisis, are you?
Dwelling over old photographs of you when you
looked like a sickening sweet Punk rock star
dressed in velvet and black leather, with splashes
of leopard-print here and there. Like, there was a
time when you were raw and mean, a time when
you had an answer for everything (a discharged
middle finger was that), a time when you may
have been smarter and wiser, with a childish
playfulness about you, which held you in its
fun-loving embrace. But today you've got a job to
uphold, people you have no choice but to please,
and your middle finger is on lockdown, bound
snugly beside its neighbors, never to be seen of in
solitude again. It's like, there was a day when life
was easy, you had it all planned out, the future
was caustic, the past was toxic, and the present was all that you had in front of you——but today
you've got bills to pay, appointments you need to adhere to, asses you've gotta kiss, and that free
world you had dreamed of when you were a rebelious teenager had gotten washed away in stacks
of paperwork piled up high on your desk. No more drunk weekends, no more stoned hollidays,
no more partying on rooftops, and no more fucking girls beneath the bridge down by the Charles
River, either——no more nothing, the life you thought you had made for yourself got sold out to
responsibilities. Yeah, dude, I can so relate. I think I'm having a midlife crisis too. It's rough!

It's ugly!
It's disgusting!
It's sick!
It's mindnumbingly dull!
It's wretched!
It's a complete fuckin waste
   of time!!!
It's **LOVE**
      LOVE
         LOVE
            IT'S JUST NOT WORTH IT

It will leave you a broken, bleeding mess
a pathetic waste of life addicted to this wretched,
fucked-up device called **LOVE**

3AM

I go to the store, the clerk
hassles me like I'm a common crook.
His dastardly smile, like he suspects
something of me—maybe he's right.
maybe, maybe, maybe
Years ago I robbed the place blind.
maybe
They didn't know what hit them.
maybe

The store clerk sees me and asks
if I need help.

I need help.

3AM

I saw the firetrucks spraying lights,
red and blue, red and blue, going
round and round, a fire in the distance
a fire in the distance   FIRE!

3AM

I buy more fuel at the store.
A couple Kickstarts and a couple
packs of cigarettes to last me
the night.

3AM

The snow falls, sprinkles down,
like I'm in a snow globe, alone,
in the dark. I hold out my hands
and whirl, basking in the snowflakes.
They surround me, like a tsunami.
I spin and laugh and frolic. I'm happy.
          alone

3AM

I feel alive, living
alone
in a dream, everything's
surreal because I feel like
I'm the last man left alive.
Everyone's sleeping and

I'm alone.

YESTERDAY
I went to this big gathering
of people.

EVERYONE wore suits and ties.

ME I dressed casual
with big-ass holes in my jeans.

SOMEONE SAYS TO ME
at least I'm not afraid to
be myself.

Am I?

Insightful Segment from
Chaos Writing:

Fucking Pissed

As we walked to the AA meeting together, I asked him how many people does it take to argue, and he wouldn't answer; so I kept pressing. Eventually I got him to say two, or maybe I said two and forced the words in his mouth, I don't know.

I explained to him that there are two sides to every coin; and he denied it. I told him that what happens is both sides dish out their facts, and it's up to us as the consumer to choose a side, to choose which facts to agree with, to choose which facts *not* to agree with; and he denied it. I explained that our culture is based on this principle, the principle of propaganda; and still convinced that he's right, he denied it.

So I asked him where did he get these so-called facts, and he wouldn't answer.

He said there's so many places.
I said tell me one.
He said I don't know where to start.
Just one, I said.

I'm so angry right now.
I'm so twisted & demented.
Nothing I say makes any sense//

This life, my world, this
eerie wet nightmare I
always find myself in
whenever I awake from
my beautific dreamscape
is so damn horrifying and
I don't want to see it
anymore.

I'm a hypocrite.
I'll be the first to admit it.

I close my eyes and try to
go back to sleep, I close
my eyes and pretend to be
somewhere else, someone
else, I close my eyes and I
try oh how I try to will
myself away from here.

when will this fall to come an end!!!

But it never works.

too soon

I feel depleted.
I'm 28-years old
stuck sucking up the fumes
of a life deleted.
I thrived and I strived for
mayhem only it came to me
when I least expected it
and the beast surrendered its soul to me
eaten and beaten
I cut through and through to the core
of my own fukking problemsssss. . . .
my own demise is coming
I'm beside myself
I'm dying and I'm trying and
I'm deciding but I'm deranged
and you know how that goes
I aim for dementia.

The world was mine::::::
but I bit off its hed
and thus I died
when my time came too late
but now it's in bed.
But
I slept with the reaper
the grimmest of grins moaning
outta pure unadulterated hate....
I lust for disaster, I desire a temper
tantrum. I live for madness
only the madness

came too soon and too soon
I became a
disaster case.
That's it I'm sold
to the highest bidder.

I'm a cliché.

I'm a poser. *Haaaahaaa!!!*

Look at me,

I've got a bloody nose.

Haaaahaaa!!!

170

Outside this guy's talking to me and telling me to slow down and that he knows I can write because his friend's got my book and that he understands getting nervous because he plays guitar and his biggest fear is breaking a fucking string onstage. But he doesn't understand because I have a disorder that actually causes me to shake and that biggest fear of his would be a terminal reality if he were me. I read something to my class on Tuesday and I had to put the paper from which I was reading down on the table because it was shaking so fast in my hand that I couldn't make out the words.

That's what I deal with.

I think people are afraid of the truth. Face it, we were born to die. Everything we do while alive is to prepare ourselves for our inevitable demise, to protect ourselves, to prolong life as much as we possibly can. But what for?—the great existential question. Why bother trying when death sits bitterly on the other side of the rainbow, waiting to take you to hell? Why do anything? We might as well just sit around and wait to die, right? Curl up into a ball and let death take us.

Why even wait for death, then? Why not just do it ourselves? Death is taking too long; I don't hear him knocking—and I have this noose that could do just fine.

Right?   Wrong!

I guess that's the part that's open for interpretation, the part where you can feel free to adlib all you want, cuz I'm not writing this story, you are! I'm only giving you the outline, supplying you with a prompt to jumpstart your career as a writer—metaphorically, of course. I can't give your life meaning, other than point out the obvious, which is you are going to die, pain and misery waiting for you in your future. Pointedness is subjective, and relying on the ideas some fuckup brings to the table, even though that is the foundation of our society, the masses absolutely dependent on the decisions of others, is foolish, downright stupid; for fuck's sake, think for yourself, and not only because I tell you to because that would be quite paradoxical—and I know nobody is reading this anyway, those who do happen to give it a second glance having tuned out by now.

That is why the world is brimming with cunts, overflowing with them—and trust me, I am no exception.

I'm fucking crazy. I mean, ca-ca-ca-cuckoo. I do shit that might seem to others as obscene, a little out there. Well, so fucking what! I don't need friends who are going to judge me. I don't judge you. I let people be, but that doesn't mean you can come around and judge ME. I make mistakes, but I'm working on my shit, and that's what counts. I admit I have problems, I'll be the first to admit it. I don't need you to point it out to me, cuz I have eyes too, I see myself when I look into the mirror, I really do. But for a friend to put me under the microscope, to analyze me, diagnose me, and then abandon me cuz they don't like what they see—fine! I don't need you anyway. I bet I could just as easily put YOU under the microscope, and I bet I'll find many things about YOU that I myself will not like; but here's the thing: I DON'T! A good way to learn to hate someone is by putting them under the microscope. And if the looking glass is broken, cracked—damaged!—what the hell does that tell you? The blind leading the blind—a whackjob analyzing a nutcase. What the hell do you think you're gonna find out anyway? Just think about it! We're all good, we're all equal, but we're all sick, it's a guarantee. So save your judgments, cuz I don't need it anyway!

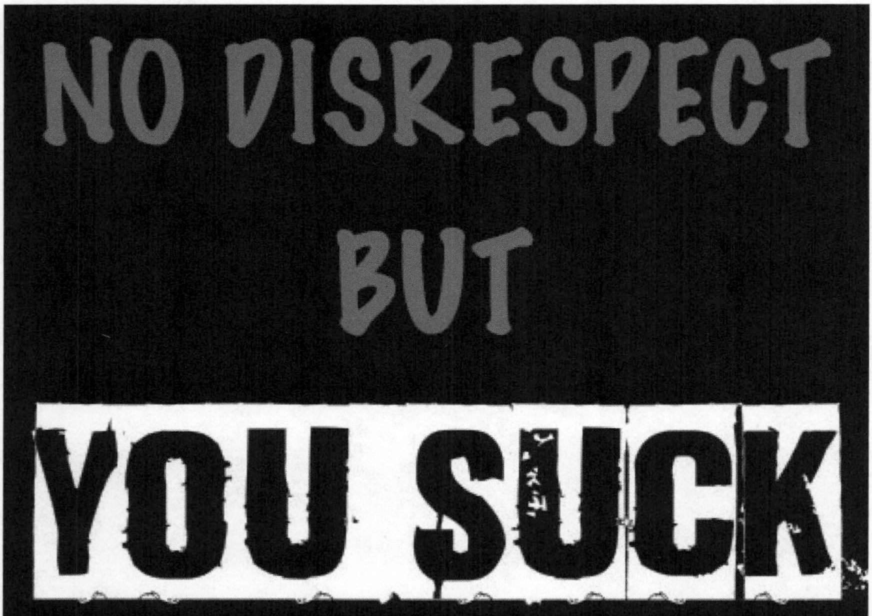
NO DISRESPECT
BUT
YOU SUCK

Niceties:

Thank you

what does it mean?

I'm sorry

people say it so much

You're welcome

are you really????

Tell that to people
whose children
don't   look   like   children
ANYMORE

How do you expect me
to sleep   at   night!

Lost & Found

I wrote a verse
here
and a box opened up
and devoured the words.
I saw each word
dissipate like
magic.
one moment they were
before me, the next
they were beyond me.

I crave disaster
got mayhem in my mind
my thoughts are fast and spastic
it's how I unwind....

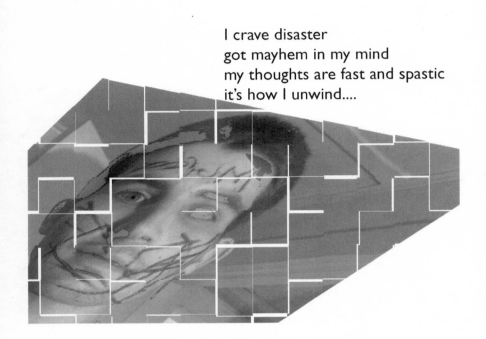

PARENTAL ADVISORY

EXPLICIT THOUGHTS

Anyone who says "Hey dude, you can't joke about that. Anything but that" is a

You're making jokes about rape, and then you're saying, "Hey, you can't joke about suicide, dude. That's not cool."

While the next person is making jokes about suicide and saying, "Hey, dude. Don't joke about rape. Not cool, dude; not cool at all."

Deeming one subject unsuitable to joke about is like sending a ball of snow down a long, steep ski slope.

It keeps rolling
and rolling
and rolling   until it gets too big to contain.
And then you end up with a dead   **DO YOU GET ME**
Mickey Mouse on your hands.   **NOW**

So Pissed

Get the fuck out of my way!

I'm wild about you

It's awesome. When I write, it's like straight-up vomiting, and then I read it months later and try to figure out what it means. It's like dissecting someone else's poem, only it's my own poems.

Evrry**1**
is N Яtist
2day

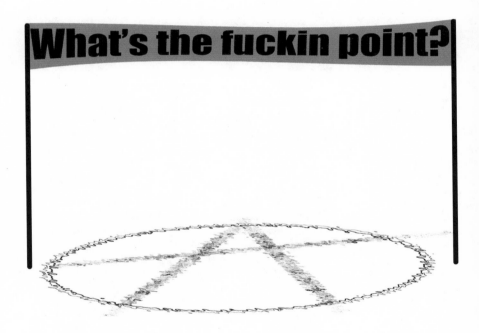

I don't know why I love you but I ♥ ➡

Like the movie *Final Destination*, I thought I saw a car crash before it happened. I wanted to shout STOP, but I was too afraid. But then the car crash didn't happen anyway, and I felt quite disappointed that I am not in fact psychic.

189

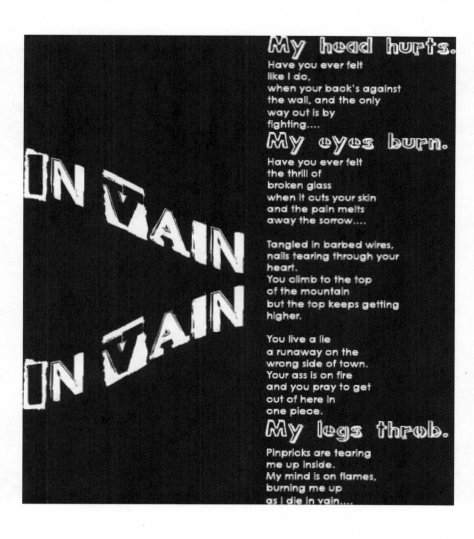

My head hurts.

Have you ever felt
like I do,
when your back's against
the wall, and the only
way out is by
fighting....

My eyes burn.

Have you ever felt
the thrill of
broken glass
when it cuts your skin
and the pain melts
away the sorrow....

Tangled in barbed wires,
nails tearing through your
heart.
You climb to the top
of the mountain
but the top keeps getting
higher.

You live a lie
a runaway on the
wrong side of town.
Your ass is on fire
and you pray to get
out of here in
one piece.

My legs throb.

Pinpricks are tearing
me up inside.
My mind is on flames,
burning me up
as I die in vain....

IN VAIN

IN VAIN

I dont know who anybody is anymore.

Facebook
screen names: Instagram
Twitter
This blog that blog
all the different gods

Goodbye religion
Hello Internet

HELL-oh MaSS MedIaa

192

But that's all right....
because I live to tell my tale,
to offer reprieve to anyone
who is amid that hell
I lived through many years ago,
in another dimension
another state of mind
another state of being
another another another....

I lived the life, I did the time,
I earned my stripes, and now
it's time to try something else
on for size

27 years old

19 years old

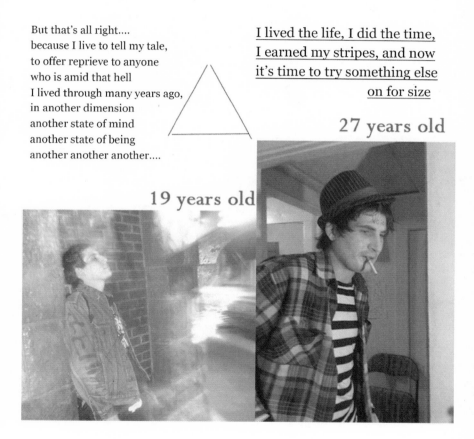

What I'm getting at is that picking sides doesn't solve any problems, all it does is create more problems. Because I choose not to pick a side people have called me apathetic or indifferent, and yet I'm the first one to hold out my hand to someone who's been the victim of persecution. Like, I got into this really heated argument with this girl who was saying I'm apathetic and I don't care because I refuse to pick a side in matters of politics, and a few months earlier that same girl messaged me in the middle of the night saying she was going to kill herself and I hurried to help her out, and I did whatever I could to keep her alive in that moment. But she forgot this fact when she was telling me I'm a bad person because I refuse to pick a side. Picking sides means I'm determining one group to be right and another group to be wrong and that just creates more problems. Everyone's like, *I'm liberal and I live by those ethics and people who don't live by those ethics are wrong.* (Nietzche said "a liberal institution ceases to be liberal the moment it is established.") Or they're saying, *I'm conservative and everyone who isn't conservative is wrong.* I mean, it takes two to tango, and choosing sides just promotes war, it gives you a reason to hate another group, an excuse to seg- regate, and what's worse is these people who are so against segregation are the first ones to divide us up. That's what I'm getting at.

195

The Old Man

I woke up.
My head hurt.
My dreams were so surreal
in the night.
I remembered lots of things
that happened, things
magically woven, like
a sweater crumpled
and burned to ashes.
My mind was on fire.
A chain of flames
swung like whiplash
and crashing into a pool of blood.
The old man sat on his blue stump.
He held a cane that looked like
a snake, the head of which
twitched and jerked in his hand.
His eyes were firm, his stare
sharp like shards of glass.
He sat there and stared numbly
up at me, like he was watching
the TV.
I looked away, trying hard
not to meet his gaze.
This man there, he stared like
he had beef with me.
Then he stood up,
cane in hand, and walked away.

The back of his head was
a mirror,
and when I looked in it,
I could not
see
myself.
What I saw was
an ominous black hole
swirling and shifting in shady
arrays, roiling violently,
with thunderous flashes showing
an ever-present skull.
I gasped when I saw it.
Gasped and jumped back.
The mirror shattered.
An explosion of glass.
The shards trickled on the ground
as the man kept walking
away from me,
fading
into
the
black.
Then he whirled,
and I woke up,
with his horrifying expression
burning my soul.
It was all I could think of
as I got dressed
and went to
work.

I'm s o in love
with her

Who
is
that girl ?

beautiful— but not in that
cliché kind of way

That Girl
I want her to be mine

my heart throbs and
pulsates   slams and whams
                    inside my chest

A PUNK ROCK SONG

There was a day when one
could speak their mind
say what they feel and tell you off
without getting a lecture about it
but I missed that day
and this day I'm here
and today I'm going crazed
and I'll bust up your face.

Don't tell me about it
cuz I don't care
Don't tell me about it
cuz I don't wanna hear it
Don't tell me about it
if you know what's good forya
Don't tell me about it
cuz I'm lost and confused and
rearing after you.

There was a day when you could
wear what you want
when you could be what you want
but this day and age freedom is lost
to TV and the Internet and other such
devices
and this day and age I'll bust up your face.

Don't tell me about it
cuz I don't care
Don't tell me about it
cuz I don't wanna hear it
Don't tell me about it
if you know what's good forya
Don't tell me about it
cuz I'm lost and confused and rearing after
you.

Kill
Kill Destroy
Destroy
Kill
Kill Destroy
Destroy

So Bored of You

Idle conversation, directionless talking, chatting and flirting, relating for the sake of relating, looking for validation, for laughs, chuckles, teeth clacking, tongues clucking, eyes wandering, rolling back into the back of my head; I'm falling asleep, slipping away into a nothingness that only comes about from sheer boredom.

I look at the clock, ticking and tocking relentlessly, staring at me from its perch on the wall—mocking me! The sound it makes is incessant, like ambient diarrhea; so irritating I wanna smash it with a rock. It moves too slowly. My mind dying, my head sinking, I'm nodding and I don't care who sees. Being here is useless; there is no gain, nobody left to save. All I see are blank faces; everybody is so blank, so utterly numb, so dumb it becomes retarded. I'm better off slapping my own chest, trying to bite off my own ear. Like a dog chases its own tail, I chase a dream, a hope, hoping things will change, be different for a change.

Insanity—doing the same thing again and again but expecting different results. I know the results, but I do it anyway. I do it because life is hopeless. I know things will never change, be the same until I die. I know the world is doomed, so coming to this place is no different than anywhere else—a pit of despair, of rot, worthless human interaction that I could do without.

i accept the fact that i fight my own wisdom , because thats what my wisdom entails — question everything . if i didnt question everything , then i wudnt be questioning everything , now wud i ? i second - guess myself way too much , always unsure , a mind never made , & that i accept . introspection is a sure way to drive a crazy person insane . act first question later ? no , i question first act never . or maybe i do act , i dont know . im at war w/ reality all the time & that i accept . it wont always be this way , i suppose , but today it is , & today i wage war on all things me . i accept myself for who i am , really i do . but who i am is someone who beats himself up too much . i dont sleep so that my mind races & races it does & in those states of racing thoughts i create art non-stop , jumping from one creative idea to the next experimental notion , & then i go to sleep , wake up the next day w/ a splitting headache , & reflect on all that i made the previous day in my hyper-aware state & i reject it all.

And That I Gotta Accept....

I like art that bites
how many times must I say it?
I love words   visceral wordplay
a fuck fuck fucking orgasm
waiting to happen.
I'm sick of positive vibes.
I enjoy   Everyone's so
chaos   damn nice.
destruction
and I want art
that explodes
in your face.

Breaking

scream   shout   chaos

it never ends
never fucking ends

202

Like
two mental cases should never
get together
unless the end goal is to

DESTROY

destroy everything cherished
Like   & cherishable
the end result of two mental
cases joined together in a
love(hate)-filled affair is

SELF-DESTRUCTION

Like
I'm incapable of loving but I love you all
the same, and for that let's go WILD

it's a mistake we all make

Insightful Segment from
Chaos Writing:

Too Quick

I don't care who you are
I don't care what you think
    what you say
    what you wear
I accept all creeds   I accept all walks of life   I'm uncouth, yes; but that doesn't mean I don't love my fellow man and want my fellow man to prosper in life.
I'm sick I have problems and sometimes
    sometimes
        sometimes I say shit without first thinking it over with
myself, sometimes I'm too quick to speak, too quick to judge, too quick …
period
sometimes I'm simply caught with my foot in my mouth….

When I wrote this post, a friend gave me some really great feedback, which he followed with, "But then, what do I know? I just like tater tots and mayonnaise"—that, right there, is the truth.
We know nothing about nothing; we all like to think we know something about something, but in the end our knowledge is moot.
    I wrote somewhere:
"We are all doing the best we can with the knowledge we think we know!"

You can't get anymore truthful than that….

I was telling someone last night that misery and happiness are a choice. For the most part I choose happiness, but there are days when I choose misery. Misery is easier, more accommodating, comfortable, familiar, and more accessible. But happiness, however, is much harder to achieve, what with growing up in Western Civilization, having been taught Western Philosophy, having been instilled Western Values: No, misery is **not** a choice; other people **can** make me angry; things outside this room **do** have the power to affect how I feel, how I think. I am a product of Western Teachings. I write about negativity because I come from dark places, I go to dark places; I got this nefarious shadow following me around and I can easily let it take me. But I don't, and I won't. So you see, I write to keep those demons away.

Nothing's right
Nothing's wrong
Feel no shame
because it's all the same.
in the end.

fight those
who fight us   fuck this shit
imprison those
who try to imprison us
arrest cops
censor left-wing extremists
gas the nazis
chain up rednecks
and drag em on the back of your trucks
bomb terrorists
and discriminate the american citizen
FUCK THE MOTHERFUCKIN SYSTEM!!!
before it fucks you

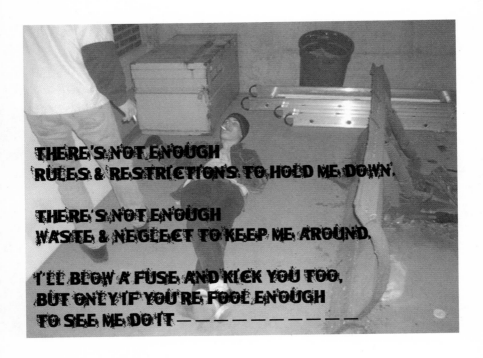

THERE'S NOT ENOUGH
RULES & RESTRICTIONS TO HOLD ME DOWN.

THERE'S NOT ENOUGH
WASTE & NEGLECT TO KEEP ME AROUND,

I'LL BLOW A FUSE AND KICK YOU TOO,
BUT ONLY IF YOU'RE FOOL ENOUGH
TO SEE ME DO IT — — — — — — — —

I WAS ALL MY FAULT

Have you ever fallen? Have you ever fallen and not stopped? Have you ever fallen and the bottom just keeps getting farther as you plunge into your own destruction....
I know I have. It's the worst, right? When you become like a sponge, sucking dry every life form that crosses your path—it's the worst....

My best friend Andrew—or my old best friend, I should say—was unfortunate enough to cross my path. Sad. So Sad, it was.

And I hate myself for it, I hate the way I ruined things, I hate the way I extracted energy and used it for my own sick purposes. It was sick.

So Sick

He had never done the stuff, he had told me. He had never done cocaine, he had explained, and What Did I Do????—I offered him a free line: Hey, here's one for free. Try this....

Try This!

This was my best friend I'm talking about—our blood strong as diamonds, our bond unbreakable, so fervent it was like it would never tear apart—or so we thought!——but it did, it broke: I went to Rutland, VT; he stayed in Haverhill, MA, and got married and had kids, and then got divorced and I can't even imagine what happened to the kids after that, probably left in the mother's own custody:
Probably ... hopefully ... but then again, she's not much more than a trainwreck herself, a drunk a bumb a loser and a mother in the 21st century.   She's just as sick, if not more, and what, 4 kids, 5 kids now, growing up in another American broken home—makes me sad, you know! The state of things.

When a door is slammed, a window is smashed, and I cut myself on the jagged glass.

I emerge on the battlefield.

Where'd everybody go? I ask as I man my rifle in a gray mist amid all the dead bodies.

The war was fought and has gone away.

With nobody left to fight I raise my rifle and press the muzzle to my—wait, I don't wanna die.

I hold onto my sanity like a crying child, patting its back and saying, *Everything will be okay.*

Spewing lies that dissipate before my eyes, I fall to my knees and cry, praying that God will take away this pain, saying, *Everything will be okay.*

I rest my head on my pillow and pray another day will make me sane—

because the war was fought and has gone away, and I'm too late.

But another day is coming and I'm running to my bed and set my head on my pillow and pray another day will make me sane, because everything will be okay.

Existential thinking turns into nihilistic conclusions. It starts with: Why am I here? what do I want? or even, Who am I? But then my hopeless outlook on life, my defeatus, fatalistic points of view, my self-depracating brain & mind that likes to hang me up in a web of pointlessness, kicks in & the answers roll right off my fingertips: Who am I? No one/// What do I want? Nothing/// Why am I here? I'm really not when I think about it. I come from the land of nowhere—isn't it grand to have such a futile outlook on life. Isn't it wonderful? No, it's nothing.   It's nothing, nowhere, & I'm no one—such fun. Today's one of those days when nothing gets done.

2 separate Xtremes = 1 messy outcome

fight for what you believe in
don't ever stop fighting
but leave room for disagreement
unless you're ready for a third world war

Is that a Joke?
Is that a Joke?
Is that a Joke?

Fireworks—a cobweb of colors,
different shades flickering in the sky.
It's a euphoric sensation,
the way your lips come in contact with mine.
Bliss—the waves of the ocean,
rolling and lapping at the sand,
water pouring from the sink faucet,
serenity when we walk hand and hand.
Noises—loud and fast and so rambunctious.
We're jumping and bumping and slamming into each other.
The guitar screams a solo, a fluctuation of notes.
We're dancing together; it's you and I forever.

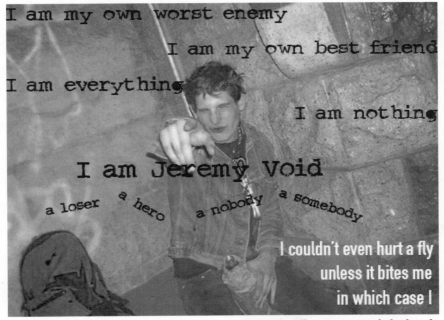

I am my own worst enemy

I am my own best friend

I am everything

I am nothing

I am Jeremy Void

a loser   a hero   a nobody   a somebody

I couldn't even hurt a fly
unless it bites me
in which case I
will be the first to smash it dead

Skewed

LOSING FRIENDS IN A DAY

Dye your hair blue.
Overnight you ve become a nigger.
Outcasted and exiled,
your fate s been made.
You search for existential purpose.
An existential reason.
Your friends turn their backs
on you, and there s nothing
you can do.

Boo hoo!

How do I turn it OFF

GO
AWAY

How do I turn it OFF

MY THOUGHTS

I'm melting

are racing

STOP!

fuck   fuck   fuck   fuck

STOP!

fuck   fuck

218

"Oh, it's on!!!"

I rarely get bored nowadays. My thoughts still race, but I've found a way to direct my racing thoughts, as opposed to letting them run rampant like the days of my past.

Shove
that
in your asshole and
watch it float....

Copy Cat Rebels

Today all the bands sound the same. I live in a small town called a city in a small state nobody gives a shit about. It's full of hippies and yo-yos and rednecks and cholos; and kids are shooting dope like it's a sport, unmarried girls are springing babies from their twats like it's a chore—a paid chore cuz the government pays them for it. I go to open-mikes to read my writing and all the performers always play rock and roll covers and there's never anything new—and when I read nobody pays me much mind cuz nobody wants new they want the same old same old. So I hang out with kids who call themselves "Punks," play in bands that have fast chord progression, quick and powerful drumbeats, and vocals that leave you with a detrimental headache what with their vicious screaming that tears holes in speakers. But I was thinking tonight—and this is why I rarely go to the shows around here or simply leave right after I read—I was thinking that I've been there done that, I've heard it all before—times a million. I've heard the sound that your voice makes as you howl into a caustic microphone, I've heard the sonic riffraff your guitar makes as you pound out power chord after power chord, the bass wobbling and wailing and the drums rumbling in a series of fact-paced thumps and crashes. I've heard it all before, and frankly I'm rather bored. It's like ... it's like they're singing the same exact songs about the bad bad government, about child rapists and lying politicians, about capitalists and the big business takeovers—white collar criminals running down mom and pop stores with their corporate bulldozers that dawn their logos on the large rolling wheels as they tumble and plow through the places of small-town business. I know this is going on, you know this is going on, so singing about this going on doesn't change a goddam thing if you ask me, it only prolongs the problem. It doesn't bring about change, especially not when a kid dressed in rags and patches and pins and studs screams about it incoherently into a broken microphone through dented speakers when only more kids who dress in rags and patches and pins and studs can hear it—kids who will listen and then start their own bands and then go and bitch and moan about it too. All it does is create more copycat bands, more mimics of rebellion, more washed-up burnt-out thick and tuneless nuisances that think rebellion means complaining to people who feel the same exact way and wanna complain about it too.

Insightful Segment from
Chaos Writing:

A Progress Report

But no, the Catholics—or any Christian for that matter—are exempt from having to do it their way, exempt from the fucking golden rule (treat others the way you'd like to be treated).

Staring down through the holes in their snotty little noses, eyes to the sky, too good to look anyone in the eye, anyone other than the others who belong to the Catholic race, who are made up with phonies and crack pots—

that's right, you're a phony!—your entire religion is based on the Roman government, don't you know?

Jesus Christ, he tried to take down the Roman government himself, but was arrested, tortured, and killed before he could succeed; and then these Romans who crucified the bastard, they wrote the fucking bible.

¿WHY?

Well I'll tell you why:

Jesus Christ was an anarchist who despised money and big businesses and all that crud; and was thus killed for fighting for what he believed in, and the Romans took the name of this great man, allegedly God's only son, and did what all modern Catholics do—exploited him.

Exploitation is the foundation of their entire religion, can you believe it!

What I think about late at night? I think about a lot of things, too much to dictate in this notebook in a timed slot of 5 minutes. I mean, late at night, my mind usually races; it jumps from one boring, oh so futile notion to the next even more boring (almost humdrum), but equally futile notion. I do my best art late at night and early in the morning cuz my scrambled brain doesn't know when to quit. It's almost like hypo-mania, per say—a racing, speeding bullet rocketing through my brain, from ear to ear, only when it reaches the other side, it bounces off that wall, almost like a pingpong ball, propelled flung swirling through time as one wave of thought crosses my mind, only to be replaced by the next, and then the next, and then the next, and so on. Like, it's midnight, I've got the Drones' song "Lookalikes" tearing out of the speakers, I'm smashing the keys of my keyboard quickly, with catlike reflexes and velocity, a poem about rage slung across the computer screen—I'm really feeling the rage, letting the rage feel me, becoming one with it, embracing it; and then, click, the song changes, and my mood sinks into an almost depression, becoming melodramatic in my wallowing as I think about her, think about Samantha, about the one that got away, the previous feelings of rage that I had felt flipped around and staring back at me—see, that's how fast I can flip a bitch!

I followed my heart and where did it get me? But fucked up with a needle in my arm. I lived fast, faster than most, but slower than the hardcore punks that I truly admired. All I wanted was more and you bet I took it I stole it and I cheated to get it and then I just took more. My life felt slippery, like I was tripping and falling flat on my face but the plunge kept getting deeper and deeper and I thought it would be forever before I connected with the ruts and stone awaiting me at the bottom of my plunge, waiting for me to splatter crash and splash all the way back to the nowhere lands. This anger and boredom and jaded sensation wrapped me up in a web of vines and I tried to break out but it only squeezed me tighter in its grasp, gripping me like a vice. This anti-passion was engrained so deeply in my veins, twisting me and driving me insane. Walking through the river against the stream I felt no pain no joy no understanding no ploy just a desire for more. ... I ripped and flailed and stabbed and yelled and I fought the devil and he fought back and I was buried alive in a grave brimming with 3-foot-long maggots nibbling on my eyes my skin my toenails and I flipped and flopped and ran and flittered and I dipped and dropped and I was going fuckkkkkkin maaddddd.

TRY NOT TO KILL ANYONE WHILE I'M GONE.

OR DO

Either way,
someone *IS* going to die tonight.

i am sure of it.

I did stupid shit
and I guess karma's a bitch.
But when I see you again
and you lose all your teeth—

well, I guess karma's a bitch.

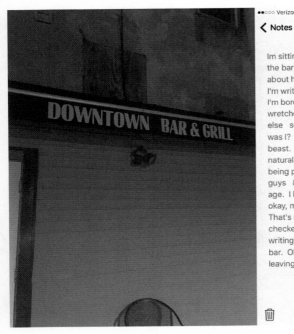

‹ Notes   ⬆

February 3, 2016 at 11:45 PM

Im sitting at the bar   I'm sober   at
the bar   sitting here   sober   & writing
about how I'm   at the bar   sober &
I'm writing about it. Okay, where was I?
I'm bored I guess. The music playing is
wretched and I wanna go   someplace
else someplace not here. Okay, where
was I? Okay, this is the nature of the
beast. This is only human nature   only
natural to be bored   while this crap is
being played   by two drunken old
guys & one sober young guy about my
age. I know his name   his name is
okay, maybe I don't. Okay, where was I?
That's right, I'm here   I'm at the bar. Last I
checked I was sipping a Red Bull   &
writing this crap   in this notebook   at the
bar. Okay, where was I? I think I was just
leaving.

🗑   📷   ✎

228

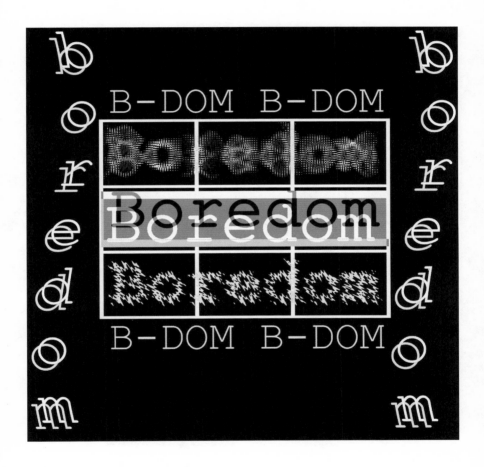

Thank God I Don't Drink Anymore

Last night I got myself in a slight bind. My ride to Burlington turned out to be a total scumbag: 1. he expected to use the money I paid him for the ride to pay some, or part, of his cable bill even though the deal was I'd pay for ALL of the gas, and nothing more, which is what I planned to do; and 2. he wanted me to sign him up for the open-mike———second-to-last, he specified———and then leave and go to his meeting at some other bar and then come back in the nick of time to read, missing all the other performers that went on before him———see what I'm dealing with here? And then he had the nerve to say that I screwed him over, me Dude he screwed himself over. He told me he was really angry with me and I told him that's on you dude, not my problem. One of the first things he said to me upon entering the car was, "I'm not in the business of saving you money"———just like how I'm not in the business of giving a shit about his feelings. Why the hell should I be?

Anyway, I'm proud of the way I handled myself. I made it out of there unscathed and I used all the tools available to me at the time. I feel like if I was drinking, even though he was the prick threatening *me*, I'd be the one in cuffs. Last night I acted mature and responsible, and if I was still amid the hell of my past, I might very well have acted immature and irresponsible. I mean, I am Jeremy St. Chaos after all, or at least I was, and today a part of him——like Dr. Jekyll and Mr. Hyde——is still inside me, buried deep down beneath my heart, and if I'm not careful enough, that side will come back up swinging——and so thank God I don't drink anymore.

230

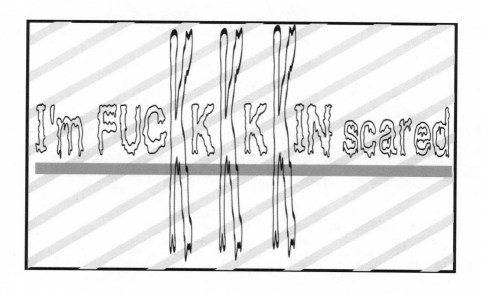

The nighttime warriors stalk the streets, boots clotting in gutters, stomping through puddles. They stand tall and mean. Black disguises and painted faces. The civilized folk stare but pretend that they don't as the street demons stroll past them and don't even care.

These are the boys

These are the girls

disillusionment run wild. Lost and troubled, they sneer, spit, and scowl. They own these streets——————the night's got nothing they can't overcome.

Seen it all before; been there done that.

From broken homes, broken lives, broken worlds collide, the whole landscape has become their playground, a sandy beach that winds through downtown and swings along uptown, spanning the face of the city, beneath the stars that stretch as far as their eyes can reach....

These are the boys

These are the girls

told of in horror stories. The few parents warn their children of, saying these kids are bad, these kids are mean, they will rob you and laugh about it later when they're with their friends.

The boys they don't want their daughters to date

The girls they don't want their sons to fuck

Lives too romantic for the likes of the suburban yuppies. Too wild for the tamed, too mean for the controlled to take. They're menaces, vagrants, young cretins wrecking havoc in this sacred town. The city burning down as these MONSTERS in black clothing come barreling down the road.

These are the kids who live next door, sinister smiles and chains galore. They creep through the city feared by the normal classes. They are doomed to a life of crime, a life of drugs, given up on by just about everyone.

These are your children for whom you turn the other cheek.

I LIKE TO CREATE ART, if you would even call it that. IF YOU DO NOT APPROVE OF THE ART I PRODUCE, by all means, UNFOLLOW ME.   IF YOU THINK ITS CRAP, well, it kind of is, dont you think.   but thats aside the point——my point is, I LIKE TO CREATE ART, end of subject.

i know that some people spend years polishing their craft, maybe even their whole lives smoothing out the edges, sanding it down and shining it all neat and tidy for all eyes to see——some people take their craft so seriously, too seriously if you ask me——some people point the tips of their noses high in the air and maybe even look down at others thru their snot holes, as if thats where they keep their eyes, hidden deep inside their noses, you know the type, they scrutinize and tell you your arts not satisfactory for the likes of them——some people are too damn high and mighty, dont do that, no you cant do that, art was never meant to be like that——some people are so proud that anything below their standards is so far from *real* art that the person responsible for said mess should be shunned by all artists everywhere, you know the kind---some people————

some people are just not REAL artists themselves....   of course, there are trolls, critics, or whatever you wanna call it, and then there are us, the ones putting in the effort, the TRUE believers....   besides, art was never meant to be taken seriously if you ask me——i mean, its not like i aspire to have my work hung up in a museum, nor do i hope to have it dangling in a gallery for all eyes to see, eyes of the more classy variety, That Is.   because my art is not classy, it will bring about goosebumps, this is true, but its not the kind of crud that others will be marveling at behind mono-cles, scholars talking in their formal drawl about how the edges and the colors and the everything else put together really bring out the message said artist is trying to convey....

if you dont like it, I dont really give a fuck, now do I?...   because I LIKE TO CREATE ART.... end of subject

THIS IS MY ART × ART × T

It's a struggle
I live in, a fight
I struggle to control
because the fight that
it is has got me under
its control

and it won't let go.

It's a hopeless struggle.

I battle its wits, I pull
out my hair before it's too late
and it's too late for this....
I won't give up, no I won't give up///

I'm living and I'm in trouble
another day another night, and it's a fight
not worth the shuffle, but I struggle by
daylight, and the dark of the night, and it
goes **bang**, it goes **bang bang**, and I'm STUCK
and I'm STUCK STUCK FUCKIN STUCKKKKK.

Let me go, I shout.
Let me out, I holler.
Just leave me alone<<< LEAVE ME ALONE....

My mental state is at risk
I'm telling you I'm in the midst
of a mental breakdown tearing and biting
and I'm pissed SO FUCKIN PISSED.

This state of mind this state of being
is beating me raw, bleeding me senseless and senseless
and I'M LOSING MY SENSE TO THIS
THIS
THIS FUCKIN BEAST THAT'S IN MY
HEAD, go **bang**, go **bang bang**, and leave
me the fuck alone, go **bang**, go **bang bang**,
and just fuckin let me go, or I'll
go **bang**, go **bang bang**, and splatter my blood
all over THE FUCKIN WALL.

MAKE IT STOP
STOP
STOP

STOOOOOOOPPPP!!!

A Hopeless Struggle

234

for this....

Pillow Talk

My life tainted
with broken aspirations that
make me feel less than
and
and
and
my life hopeless
my world broken
my existence floating away on a wisp of smoke
and
and
and
if only I could see her again
be embraced as she kisses me deeply
the girl of my dreams
and
and
and
it's a worthless struggle
step back and give up
as life shimmers past me dissipates and is gone
and
and
and
it's gone

Where am I????

Let's see

GO!!!

Help

I'm stuck

NO NO NO

Follow the LEADER

going down

237

238

239

Life As a Poet

in RUTland, VT

I'm bored.

Let me see: I'm at the Center Street Alley—open-mike night—conspiring to ride up to Burlington Tuesday night with a few older guys for another open-mike, but of the spoken word variety.

I'm bored.

Let me see: Before me four grown men are whacking balls with long, wooden sticks, and then the balls roll and spin, skittering and clacking as they connect with another set of balls on the other side of the green-matted, rectangular table.

I'm bored.

Let me see: I can hear the metronomic thrumming of a bass guitar being plucked rhythmically and emotionlessly, I can hear the monotonous sound of communication being exchanged gingerly from one person to the next, and I can hear the steady beat of my own heart as it tells me to leave, GET OUT WHILE YOU CAN!!!, and I rise to my feet, lift my bag and toss it over my back, and make a B-line straight for the door.

243

im a nihilist
I believe in NOthing
but then there's something
out there beyond me
There has to be, and I pray to
it
what is it?
A Dream, a Scheme, it's got me
tied to the magazines
of love
This love

I JUST GOT
BETTER THINGS TO DO!!!

Everybody turns on you. You do the right thing but it doesn't matter—nothing matters. You feel numb and alone, dumb and blind—nothing matters anymore. What's the point when they hate you? You try and try but your tries are worthless. It's like you're 5-years old again. You're running away. You're stuck in a rut and you're running ... running ... *somebody help me please i dont know whats going on im scared & alone please help me.* Darkness seizes you. You've done the right thing, but to what does it matter? You're giving up, you're breaking down down down—you're lost and alone, stuck and so very sold. Falling—that's your anthem. Falling into damnation ...

Your image shatters and it's over from here....

er from here.... Your image shatters and it's all ov

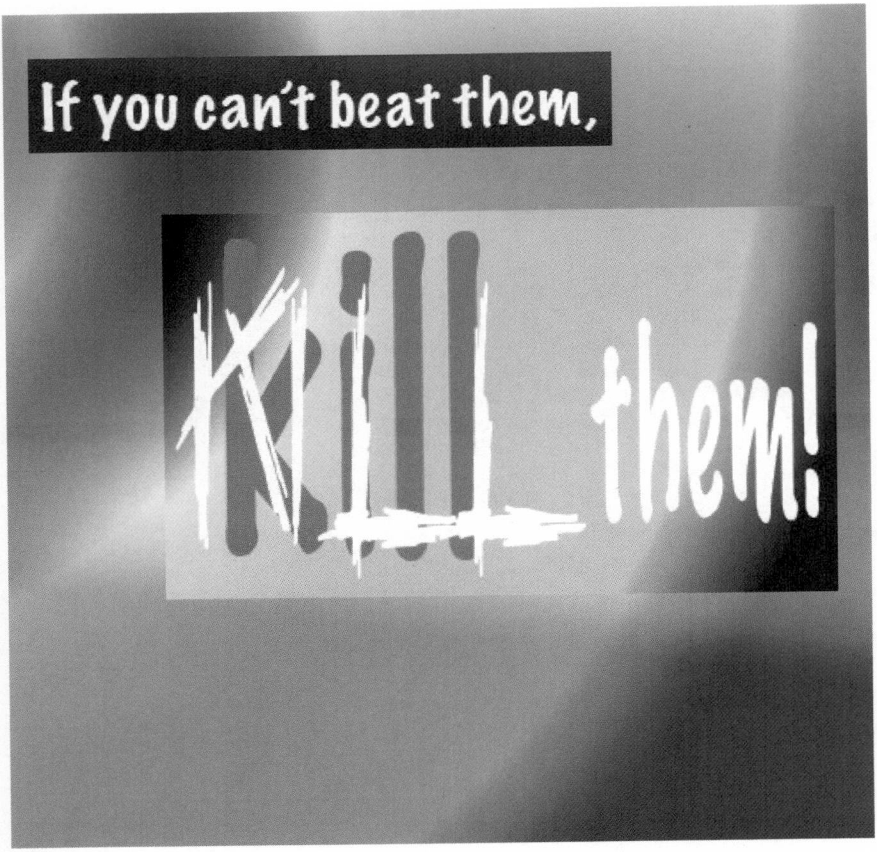
If you can't beat them,
Kill them!

Time   &   En-

Aaaa aaaah   ergy

WASTED

breaking apart
until things upon?

falling

falling

falling

Get
Me
Out of here

crashing

The story of my life

I'm too smart to follow

. . . .too stupid to lead

<u>Welcome to the 21st century</u>

This girl asked:
Why doesn't anyone love me?

I wrote:
Because it's the 21st century.

Then:
Love doesn't exist anymore.

What, it's the truth!

Right now the world is broken, and I fix it with the blunt edge of a
sledgehammer. Right now the world is shattered, and I fix it with
the crisp point of a pick axe.

Really, I don't know. Life is happening and I just don't know. I
squander this universe in search of some sort of answer, but the
only answers I ever get feel like razor blades against my skin---

razors dipped in lemon juice, that is.

Right now the world is fractured, and I fix it with the heel of my
boot. The world is damaged, smashed up, trashed, and glimmering
with disuse. I stand in the crossfire

I stand in the traffic jam, in the haphazard assortment of nothing.
I stand amid the mayhem and I scream

I scream as loud as I can---

This is life. Right now I can honestly say I'm demented, disor-
dered---demented disordered and deranged---and I piece my brain
back together with the stammering blade of a jackhammer.

Right now the world is   FUCKED   UP!!!

The fucking faggot put his hands on me at the bar and
started feeling me up. So I pushed him away. He goes,
"Why'd you push me off you like that?" I go, "Because
you were feeling me up. That's gross." He goes,
"That's not cool." I ignore him. Then he says, "Do you
know who I am?" I say, "No, and I don't care." He
goes, "You don't know who I am?" I say, "No, should
I?" Let me back up for a minute. First he comes up to
me, leans in close, and says, "Put your books down
and talk to people." I say, "No." He goes, "This is a
bar, so get up and talk to people." I say, "I'm enjoying
myself right here" and he says finally, "Well I'm enjoy-
ing you." Then the above happened, and moments
later I picked up my books and left.

Keep Youя hAnds offa ME

Or plan to get your face
kicked in, OK????

I DON'T CARE IF YOU'RE THE HEROIN KINGPIN OF
RUTLAND, keep your fucking hands off me.

I LOOK but I dont TOUCH

WHY? because I'd _much_ rather TOUCH myself!

253

I had this friend named Swilly, or Swilly Dog as some might call him, younger brother of Lost Dog—a crazy bunch, if I might say so. They were travellers, hopped trains, hitchhiked, walked a lot, they'd been all over the country, sometimes together, sometimes alone. When I first met Swilly he was alone. I had no idea he had a brother then. I think he hooked up with my ex-girlfriend Samantha that night, or some night soon after; they only made out, I was there—we weren't together at the time, only friends. Well, anyway, one night on the train—Samantha was there, Swilly was there, a bunch of Samantha's friends, other "Punks" from the scene, who didn't like me much because I was too destructive and I didn't like them much because they weren't destructive enough, were there too—Swilly Dog, a guy who knew just about everyone on the scene, he turns to me and says, You know, you and Samantha are probably the only two Punks left in Boston. This from a guy who a few days or weeks prior had told me that Punk rock is pulling razorblades out and bringing them into the moshpit—that's his reference point of what true Punk rock is. I guess according to him I'm that crazy. I once brought a rock the size of my head into a moshpit during some backyard show behind this young guy's house—that definitely didn't end so well. Let me tell you: I smashed open my own fucking kneecap with that thing, true story; just toppled onto my side on the sidelines with a bummed knee. But my band still went up and played our set shortly after, and I was still batshit crazy as the frontman of a batshit crazy band.

But that's not my point. My point is, although I've been very reckless and dangerous in my past, I've always been a thinker—*that's* my point. In fact, thinking is what fueled my reckless behavior in the first place. But here's the thing: most "Punks" these days don't know how to think. The Subhumans are telling you to think, UK Subs are saying fucking think for yourself, Crass are saying, DON'T OBEY. Wake up and THINK for a change. These mindless drones in their useless uniforms that they got off of E-Bay for who knows how much, are parading around like hot-shot toughguys. When Punk became just another macho scene for toughguy turds was the day that Punk rock died, I'm sorry to say. All these bands sing about jocks pretending to be Punks so they can bully us from the inside, and all these dipshits listen to those bands and they probably don't even hear the words but only the music because music doesn't make you think, words do!

I guess that's one of the advantageous of living in Rutland, VT: the Punks here, or at least the real ones, do like to think, they do appreciate art, and they're usually good for a deep, stimulating, intellectual conversation. In a big city, though, where there are much more open minds, you are more likely going to attract crossovers. Whereas in Rutland, a small city closed off to any differences, only the True Believers hang around.

254

I'm bored
I'm a good person

I'm bored
Why do you hate me

I'm bored
Can you relate with me

I'm bored
I tried   but I failed

That's just the way
that it goes
for me!

Solution:
Piss Everybody OFF

Hate, anger, rage are all agents of change. Without discomfort nothing would get done. We'd stay stagnant, which in my opinion is worst. That's what this world has devolved into: animals so obsessed with love and thinking love is awesome and we need nothing else, but look where it's got our society—apathetic, hopeless, and in love. I love you, I think you're perfect, and I never want you to change. Or I hate you, you're terrible, and I see your flaws. I get you gotta accept others for who they are, cuz they might not want to change and that you gotta accept. But as a whole, this world needs more anger, hate, and rage. It's what makes the world go around, it makes us learn and grow and become better people.

Pledge Allegiance to . . . what?

I'm lost in a corrupted world
in a broken society
in the land of the free
the home of the brave
          or so they say.

I'm lost in tomorrow's world
in yesterday's society
in the land of the broke
the home of the pompous
          or so they preach.

I'm stuck in this twisted world
in an assbackwards society
in the land of the fat
the home of the _____
          I'm going to sleep. . . .

A tug of war going on in my head....

A mental push-and-pull....

A cacophony of words tearing through my head....

Violent discourse like 2 sides spewing lies is spinning around my head, making me dizzy and fed up, sick and lost and in a world of my own, thought bubbles growing and popping and spraying me in the eye with intellectual jive, too fast for me to comprehend, so fast that I wish I was dead.

The Flame Dance

The flame dances as death comes nearer.
The electricity coursing through keeps it alive,
and getting dearer.
The other candle, the one representing life—
the life I have, the life that's dying—
it fades out and is forgotten about.
The death flame grows and glowers.
The life inside me ebbs as I suck in
another drag.
Another cup of coffee, another bad habit.
Another wasted day, and the death flame leers.
It dances in laughter, taunting me.
The flame of life is snuffed ... out.

I'm torn.

I want to be myself and please no one.

Yet I'm obsessed with LIKEs and the public opinion.

I'm confused.

Should I say fuck you and move on with my life?

Or should I shake your hand, even though I really want to stab you in the back.

Should I listen to your vile and pretend that I care, just so that you will read my vile and pretend that you care?

If My Love was talking it would tell me to open this door, but knowing my history with My Love I oughta keep that door shut. *C'mon, honey. Open up, I've got a surprise for you on the other side.* I stare at said door, listening to the ticking go off in my head, tick tock, I count the minutes, the seconds, I watch the door sitting there all stagnant-like, unmoving, just waiting for me to open it and step inside.

But I've ventured down this road many a time; I know what waits for me on the other side---nothing good, that's for sure. My Love, or Succubus as some might call her, is chiding me to go forth, to crank the nob, wrench it open, and go inside. But I'd rather not.

"*Everybody's happy nowadays*" sang the
Buzzcocks in the late 1970s.
"*Everybody's happy nowadays*" is a
thought that is known to frequent
my mind in, oh, the year 2016
2015   2014   etcetera etcetera.
Nothing's changed—everything the same.
The Streets are polluted
with liars—phonies——actors and the like.

PRETENDERS
pretending everything is great.

But nothing is great.   It's all the same.

It's all so   fake.   FAKE>>>>>

I want out.
I want out.
I want out of this cage.

Nihilsim Reality

It's like, nothing's real; but everything, it all feels like it's there. In front of me. I reach my hand out and touch it, and—*poof!*—it disappears.   It was never there to begin with.

My reality is only a mere disillusion. It sits there all wonderfully beautiful, but when I will it to go bye-bye, it up and leaves—   just like that. Isn't life fun?—I'd say. It's fun, but it sucks. It sucks like that whore I picked up in the green-light district, or was that light orange.   Either way, I'm frequently finding myself quite bored.

I could fly and be happy too, you know—just lift my wings and scoot upward, straight into the sky—   but physics can be quite a bitch at times, but only because I believe it to; but without it all things are possible: but but but....

But——nothing!

I knew this girl once she hated me. But I changed her mind—boy did I! She fell for me hard and would tell me everyday before she got off the phone that she loved me. I said nothing. She should have still hated me; I know I would have if I were in her shoes; but she was delusional, her reality diluted with butterflies and flowers. She fell for me and landed on her head; I wasn't there to catch her.   When we met she had thought I was a scumbag: she told that to my best friend.

When asked I said the reason I never say I LOVE YOU back is because I don't, and just like that I got off the phone>>>>

We broke up because I loved whiskey more than her, is what I had told her before she slapped me five times in the face and then walked off into the night.

It's just funny how we perceive reality and how reality tends to deceive us.

self-destruction

mental annihilation

K
  I
    L
      L yourself **now**

                                        is a dream

                                                that

                                I strive for

try on this thought-murdering device
wear it like a badge of honor
be proud of your mindlessness

                    because we only die

TOO STUPID
                    once
TOO THICK
TOO IDIOTIC
TOO RECKLESS AND RETARDED

DoN't ThInK aNyMoRe

....with friends like you

I don't know you too well (I wish I had a chance to know you better but I don't see that happening anytime soon), and so I can't say whether you're good enough or not. But I can say this: you're as good as you let yourself be. If you measure yourself by how well someone touches you, you're neglecting other factors such as this person may very well not be good enough for you and as a result their touch wasn't satisfactory. But you have the right to feel angry, I understand that; I get angry all the time, and anger is a great thing because anger is a result of something not being right in your life, and when things are not right you've either gotta fix it or accept it. I always tell people that anger is a great thing; personally I consider it a virtue, and sometimes I would consider love a vice because we hide behind love and happy feelings almost like it's a cop-out, just another way to escape; and when you're feeling angry, it means the truth is starting to sink in and you've gotta do something about it. Anger is a motivator; love is a pacifier. Our government wants us to love each other; our whole modern day society is built on love, because if we love we'll never want anything more. Sorry I'm in kind of a philosophical mood right now, so I apologize about the rant here. But either way, let yourself feel whatever you're feeling and don't fight it, just let it run its course, embrace it while it's here.

When someone says:

"You know, Jeremy, sometimes you're really hard to figure out. Sometimes I wonder if you really are as [blah blah blah] as you say you are."

I don't know why I try.

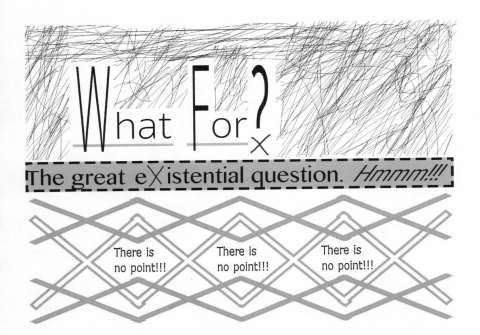

What For?

x

The great eXistential question. *Hmmm!!!*

There is no point!!!   There is no point!!!   There is no point!!!

You were born into a world in which people, everyone you meet, would stop at nothing to change you, to make you just like them. Condition you to think, act, and feel in sync with the mass majority. The quote-unquote "normal" folk who get along with others easily, like it's their vocation to, like they were born with a second brain—a brain that feeds them knowledge, awareness, an understanding which you don't seem to have, my friend. They mingle with ease, and you struggle with such a thing, and they only want you to cooporate, which, unfortunately for them, is not engrained in your DNA. You will not, CANnot, cooporate. It's not hard-wired in your blood

This is your time to rise above the social construct and shout that you will not fucking take it anymore; you will not be the system's puppet!

271

Once in court I saw this carved into the back of a bench:

If you want the judge to get you off, have her blow you!

I would have taken a picture of it but I guess I didn't think of it then.

The one that got away

Dismissed

Oh how I miss that girl
the one that got away
sank into my skin
like a spike
A drooling tragedy
I'm walking backwards
nearer to
a better day, but now
the days are getting louder
everybody's shouting
I scramble through the crowds
all pointing and laughing at me
I cover my head
as the needle punches through
my heart.
world's apart
Oh how I miss her
oh how life goes on
and on
and on

and my heart
it jumps ebbs and stops
restarts . . . this dreamscape
oh how I long
for escape
Oh how I need something more
and more
and more
but the answers never come
when I'm awake.
A pinch   a poke
my head is sinking
my mind is driftng
my eyes are seeping
my conscious slipping fast
as I float away
into an epic oblivian.
Oh how I miss   that   girl ...
beep   beep   beep

beeeeeeeep!

Sometimes

I'll be walking down the street and then see somebody whose face I wanna punch, or who I have the sudden urge to push out in front of a truck.

These thoughts  I can't always control them, you know.

Some people

might call me evil.   A bad person.

But then,

Who The Hell Are You????

What The Hell Have You Done??   Huh!

An idea
strung from
an idea

If it was up to me
I'd reach outward
and reach inward
and rip out
your brain and eat it and

        If it was up to
        me
I
'd do a lot of things.

For one I'd
have my own throne.
A throne I'd build   myself
because I am God and you better
hate me or
love me
or be damned////
One or the other
it don't make a damn
difference to me.

As long as you feel something..

As long as you know I exist
that's all I'm saying.

All I 'm saying is I like
that idea and
I wish it was mine
and and and
   and

Period.

The end of a dream
is wetter than the dream
itself....
To cum in your sleep
is like cumming in
The World real.

Do you knooow me.
Do yoou know me me.
Do you listen to me
rant   a lot because
that's all I seem cap
able of doing these days   these days..

My life is backwards I died first.
I died and then was revived.
I lived from the olden age
to the golden age
and then climbed back into the womb and

went to sleep! ... I

Have you ever lived like that?
Have you ever lived like I did.

A boy sent to destroy
A boy taught to avoid
from day one.

I was that boy
and I did destroy
          a lot of things
and avoided
The World real.

That's why they call me Void
or Jeremy for short

or

J-Void   that works too.

Call me whatever you want
as long as you don't know
my real name
and I can

still get that job.

That's all I want
to be a productive
member
of
our society.

Work and make money
Work and eat and
make money.

Money is everything
in

The World real.

I DON'T KNOW I DON'T CARE
I DON'T BOTHER I DON'T TRY

I want to be
a revolutionary.
I want to have a cause.
I want to fight the system.
I want to break the law.

I beat my head against the wall
until my skin rips starts spitting blood.
I go and dance the pain away in
a terroristic fashion.
I go out with the crowd
but they all bore me and I wanna
do something else instead.

I sit back and wait
for something big to happen.
But I sit here all day long
and nothing seems enough.
My mind races through blackness
as I contemplate the sky.
The rainbow has sprouted blood
and the evil birds are flying.

The whole world is
immersed in flames
and I don't know what to do.
I wait for action to be made

but it all seems way too late
to be of any use.

I'm ignorant and undereducated
and refuse to listen to
what you have to say.
Because your knowledge is worthless
to a kid like me who would
only go out and abuse it.

So why don't you go away,
cuz I'm a good for nothing
kid who belongs on a different planet.
If you ask me what's my name,
I'll make up something sick
and cram it down your face.

I don't know why
I'm even writing this.
I guess just killing time.
If I had something smart to say,
they might put me away for good.

i look at a photograph of me
my hair charged & black like charcoal
my eyes red like diamonds
my lips screwed up, cringing w/
         utter disgust
i see the resemblance, intellectually;
i can easily point out the similarities.
but if you ask me

         IF YOU ASK ME
who this man is, id tell you,
NOT ME   i dont feel this mans
aura, i dont feel a connection.
its like i stepped into a new dimension.

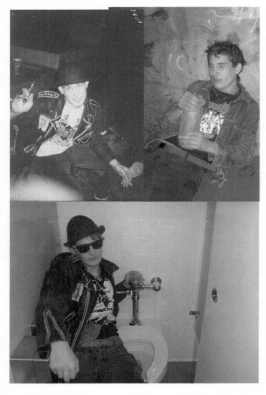

this man is lost, a victim of his own sick lust.
i was found, years ago, &
had evolved into something so much more
                         than that

         Sure, he & i are the same
         we share the same heart,
         only this mans heart—

it was all mangled & gross
gutted & tangled, whereas my own
has been stitched back together. i feel like
a whole new person, & i dont seem to
recognize this image of the past anymore.

it seems so far-fetched to me.

ARTIST 2 ARTIST

Can you relate?

I really hate hate hate

existing

I wanna disapear
crawl into a hole
and never come out AGAIN

Nothing GOOD
can come from this life

I try & I try,   but for what ????

ARTIST 2 ARTIST

Can you relate with me?
useless
it's useless anyway
We're all dying anyway useless
and soon I'll be dead and buried six feet
into the ground

279

This is the way I feel

This is who I am

I come from a world most people wouldn't believe existed

YOU MADE ME

who I am
and that you'd just never understand

Comb your hair
Brush your teeth
Dress up
Make yourself look all neat
neat
neat

But who am I trying to impress????

not**me**
cuz I could care less.

I'm doing everything I can to make the world a better place. More than most people, at least. It's not that people are lazy or blind or just asleep, it's that people simply don't care one way or another, and no one is going to make them care. And not to mention that people are lazy and blind and sleeping while the world goes to hell around them. The common consensus of most Americans seems to be: *The walls are burning down around us. Where's the gas tank? Let's make this building REALLY burn to the ground!*

I've got a lot of experience with suffering too. I've suffered at the brunt of society countless times. From jocks bashing me till I'm broken and bloody. Teachers harassing me till I'm sick and distraught. Cops slamming me into walls and threatening to break my skull, prodding me with clubs and long, steel flashlights. Parents comparing me to siblings and punishing me because I'll never be good enough. Girl using me till I'm blue and humiliated. The fucking judge racking the mallet against the hardwood bench and sending me off to somewhere just to endure one more fucking year of senseless torment. POs hammering me, doctors badgering me, nurses pointing fingers and orderlies tying me up and sticking needles into my ass. Ever had a catheter shoved into your dick hole when you're completely conscious of it? The most fucking humiliating fucking thing I've ever been through, and nearly the most painful. I know what suffering is, trust me. But I don't fucking care about any of that. Because if anything, I'm glad that it happened to me, it gave me a greater knowledge and understanding that most people seem to lack.

282

Do everything I wouldn't do

and everything I would do;

in fact, do it all

because we only DIE once.

Live fast, die young

A N D

leave an ugly corpse.

We do it
because
we do it

We're fed garbage
We're fed rotten fish
We're bred to not
think
or act.

Thinking is a crime
in this state
in this day and age.

The thought police come bounding down
the road swinging their clubs
and getting ready to discharge
their tazzzers
at any given moment.

They stand there tall and tough
wearing their badges which don't
mean nothing ...
to me.

They are my
ENEMY

We stand there—

Wait   where'd everybody go?

I'm alone on the frontline
alone in the field
with fifty-one pigs marching
toward me
in my direction.

with guns and shields
and clubs that are real
ly rugged and tough.

I stand alone
a rebel alone is still
a rebel but
a dead rebel
whose blood is splattered on
the tracks beneath the Tank.

I feel like I'm
the only one fighting
at times.

I feel like I'm
the only man
or woman I might add
that gives a damn
anymore.

You talk of freedom
and peace and freedom
and joy and happiness
but where were you?
when the shit hit the fan....

Where were you?
when the guns went off
the rockets fired missiles
MADE IN AMERICA
that whistled through
the dark red sky.

Where were you? when
the riots started and people
were shot for the
color of their skin.
Tsk tsk tsk.

And where was I?

At home writing THIS

I heard—so dont quote me on it—that Webster Dictionary changed the definition of "literal" to mean metaphorical, like "I could literally eat a horse"—a metaphor. But—and heres the biggie—if literal means metaphor, then the metaphor is no longer a metaphor.

 is our world

is the society that we live in

Last night I watched a stand-up comedian tell jokes on Netflix Instant in front of a live audience. Except for maybe one or two clever statements, the jokes were rather lame—just spraying obscenities out of his mouth as much and as quickly as possible. But—and heres the biggie—the crowd before him was eating it up. Like, at the mention of his uncle sucking a tiny dick, everyone broke out laughing like it was a virus of some kind.

TRUST NO ONE

NEGLECT RESPONSIBILITIES

RUN AWAY HIDE INSIDE

Be a closet case   before it's too late/

a1,   a2,

and a 1-2-3-4

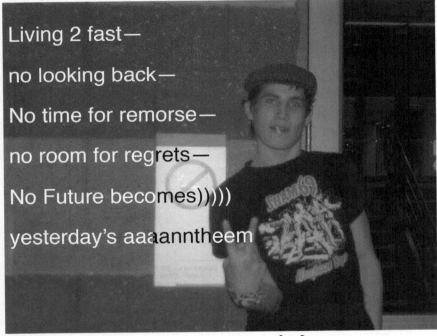

Living 2 fast—

no looking back—

No time for remorse—

no room for regrets—

No Future becomes)))))

yesterday's aaaanntheem

{silence—song ends}

Insightful Segment from
Chaos Writing:

Sicko

For me, the thought of fondling a young boy makes me sick to my stomach—yuck!——
and the thought of fondling a young girl who hasn't even developed mosquito bites on her chest yet makes me feel equally sick, like I'm in fact a sick person. Granted—and I *will* admit this shamelessly—I *have* checked out younger girls who are currently coming into their own—I mean, who hasn't?—but it's all blanketed with the thought I wonder what she will look like when she gets older, will she be hot and fuckable? or a fat cow who deserves no attention from her peers? or a pimply-faced cretin like my first girlfriend, whose tits were lopsided and whose face was crooked——probably the first of the three, considering that the girls in question always look like dolls already, so sweet and wonderful in their pink sweatpants and baby-blue blouses.
I mean, it's so hard to not fall in love with one of these girls when getting to know them; but trust me on this, I would never, ever cross the line with that kind of thinking, I would never molest or rape one of these prim examples of beauty in this ugly, rotten world—*I would never!*

It's just so wrong/
so sick/
so   *immoral////*   Like I said, I don't even fantasize about being with a young *girl,* let alone a boy; I limit my thinking to only mere speculations about what she will look like when she gets older—when she throws away her ratty old training bra and replaces it with a real one————*that's it!*

287

The world is falling apart
                piece by piece
I sit in the ashes and watch
    as they all kill each other
I wait quietly because
                my time is coming
Terror is in my midst
I bathe in the madness
        bask in the glory
the world is coming apart
    stitch by fucking stitch
and I sit in the dark
    clenching the knife
            cradling the gun
    waiting for something
        waiting for my fun
and it is done

 it's fucking done

I want everyone to read
this poem.
I'll shove it in your face
if I haveta.

Better yet, I don't want
you to read it.
Because maybe then
you'll sully it with your
ugliness.

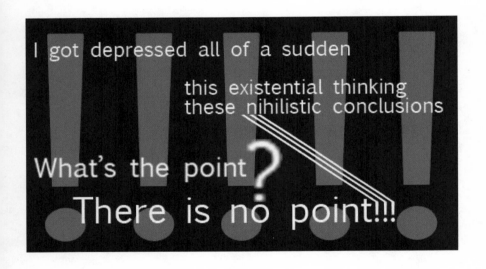

When you just got nothing to do

when you simply have nothing to lose

when your world is getting smaller by the minute

the sustenance of your life lessening and going extinct

it's <u>liberating, isn't it?</u>

When Boredom strikes

When Madness bites

When the cold spike of the night

cuts through me like

an ice pick

I will fight
I will live my life

I won't look back

Verbal War

Words are my ammunition.
My weapon of mass destruction.
I use them wisely,
and buildings erupt beneath me.
I see the Ozone burning down around me.
A riot ignites, and bodies fly.
Walls collapse beneath my tongue.
It clucks and the whole world collapses in on itself.

I see madness boiling in your eyes.
I see an explosion roiling in your mind.
I see an erosion of hellfire. People dying.
I see what you are, and I try to stop it
before it's
too
late.

Verbal War

This is my time.
This is my day.
This is your demise,
because I will rise above it all.

I see nastiness gutted and chucked.
I see fat fucks fucking a duck.
I see babies yanked from the twats of their mothers
by men in green robes and tinfoil on their heads.
The world is going to shit in a hand basket
and we try to stop it but get pulled down in the process.

Help a drowning man swim and see
what happens.
Defuse a flailing man on flames.
You're insane if you think there's a solution.
You're insane if you think
you can stop it
before it's too late.

And it's too late.

where am i going ? i am going somewhere , hopefully , but probly nowhere . i want to go anywhere , be anyone , & do anything ; but chances are , as history has shown time & time again , the floor will rise up fast & smack me in the jaw . im heading that way , way downward , into a downward plunge . the wall wont break my fall this time , ill go crashing straight thru , an eruption of concrete as i continue my descent .

where am i going ? you ask . i thrust my index finger out in front & say , NOT THERE ! i know youll be quite perplexed by my response , for i am rather perplexed w/ my reaction . i wanted to say , That Way ! i wanted to say , Im Going That Way , but you know , i never do get what i want .

truth be told , i want success . but what is success ? for me its the absence of a bottle , the lack of chemical stimulants , chemical downers . i only need life to bring me down , thats all . but ill need something to lift me back up , thats for sure .

i want more than what the promises guarantee ; i want a life that doesnt revolve around the removal of something , but a life that obtains anything . i dont want anti-goals , i want real ambitions .

but i have none , so its easier to hope for something not to happen . easier than wishing it wud . but all this wishful thinking will only bring me down , & like i sed , ill need something to lift me back up . something that i cant have . something that is dangerous in my hands .

so im stuck . im stuck fucked & it sucks . i want something , really i do , but the only thing i can think of in this dire time of wanting will make the ground tip sideways & again the wall will break my fall , but it wont .

& so i give up .

& so its no use .

& so i stop wishing & start living for a change . now , theres an idea .

I'm yearning for a yesterday that will never come.

I'm dreaming of a tomorrow that is already gone.

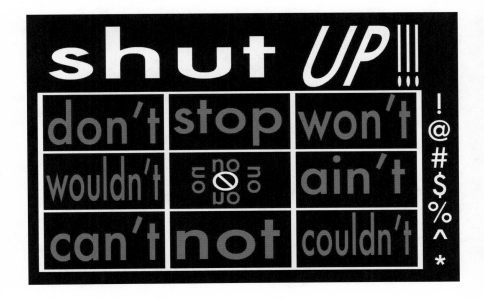

297

298

What's with this common belief that we have to be someone or something? Why can't we just exist? Accept the nothingness or worry endlessly that our purpose has yet to be fulfilled?

Which is easier to do?

Anyone Doing Anything Right

Bathing Oneself in Words

Words
to me
are
I like
use soap.
them
to
cleanse
my soul.

going crazy crazy crazy
MADD

Sins are good
sins are great
The God we believe in
is all for vices.
He says
kill the wife
Kill the children
All is good as long as
you kill someone.
Steal rape and get fat
cuz all is good in God's land.
Fight others of different creed.
Beat them down and make em bleed.
Sinfulness is godliness
or at least that's what the Bible says.

Tell me something ::::::

Why do you hate me??

Did I do something wrong?

Did I step on your toes?
or something

C'mon,
I need to know!

I'm not a bad person.
I'm really not

I swear to GOD!

I'm only human

and
I've made my mistakes.

YES it's true...
But so FUCKing what?

I wear steel-toes just for kicks.
I dress in a way that'll make you sick.
I go around acting like a total prick.
    And I do it all just for kicks

doom

the inevitable looms
ahead of me like a
stop sign but i do not
yield. i keep pushing forward.

Insightful Segment from
Chaos Writing:

Punk Rock

Plus, these kids, fellow Punk rockers, are some of the most honest, genuine kids I've ever met. If you would just put down your prior assumptions and give us a chance, you might be surprised, you might learn a thing or two, come to find out that the things that bump in the night are in fact smart and interesting and have so much potential——more potential than your own wonderful kids who you tend to put on the pedestal and brag about all the good they do, about the fact that they are so good at falling in line, following rules, and kissing ass.

Where does that ever get anyone?

A lifetime doomed to be jammed inside a tiny cubicle.

Sounds like hell to me….

So this Punk rock, this thing you hold in such low regard, made me a better person, without it I'd be even more of a clueless fuckup than I already was.

Without Punk rock I would have killed myself, and with all your closing down venues and trying to keep us off the streets, my blood would have been on you….

Now, sit on that!

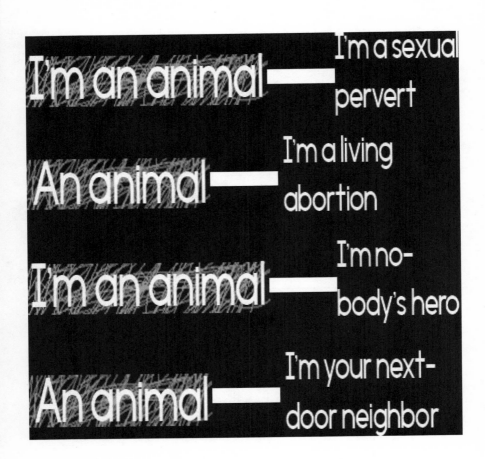

I'm an animal — I'm a sexual pervert

An animal — I'm a living abortion

I'm an animal — I'm nobody's hero

An animal — I'm your next-door neighbor

310

If I could say anything
just one thing
to tear into your mind
rip through your soul
beat your heart before it beats you

If I could spell it out
turn the world around with
the perfect words
which will lift you up
and twirl you
hurl you into the stars

When the night is right
and my mind buzzes
frightened disgusted lost
I sometimes have it there
bring it here
spit it out and it always
comes out sound
so sound
it goes way over my head

If I had the perfect words
the perfect verse

a line to save the world from itself
to change your mental health
to rip you open
lick you and suck you
and fuck you till the world melts

If I could speak to you so softly
that you would bleed for me in a coffin
rotting in the ground like a dirty crown
wrapped around your head, wrapped
in barbed thorns that stab you deep
deep in the brain

If I had the magic words that could
bring about change
the perfect rhyming line
that would end all war
end all fighting, all famine

perfection at its very worst

If I had those characters
the symbolic English letters
that would heal you

I might just stop writing....

Remember what happened last night?
Neither do I

Last night I had a dream about soggy hotdogs encrusted with raspberry jelly and I ate the hotdogs, got jelly smeared all around my lips, and with a napkin I wiped the jelly away but ... *poof!* ... the napkin turned into a giant lizard growing larger and larger by the minute. I stepped back in shock as the lizard reached epic heights. It looked me in the eye and said, Jimmy!—some reason in the dream my name was Jimmy—it said, Jimmy Boid, and cocked its head back with striking speed and precision and with that its necked crunched which made me think of thick, hairy strands of confetti; I don't know why, it just did. And out of its eyes came these silver lavish rays that hit the ground and cut straight through. The giant lizard, looming over me with silver laser beams spraying from its eyes, it said, Dance for me, Jimmy. So I danced. I danced nervously; just wobbled and tapped my feet to avoid the menacing sting of those bright silver rays as they zoomed straight toward me, aiming to hit me but my feet were too quick and slippery; or maybe he was just trying to frighten me, I don't know. So I danced and lasers came at me and then stopped suddenly and the lizard cocked its head back again and let out a deep, hollow guffaw that echoed in the mountainside. Did I mention I was in the mountains? Well, I was in the mountains, probably during the days of the Wild West, cuz I noticed I had two six-shooters holstered at each hip and I drew the one on my left with my right hand as fast as lightning, pulled it straight out, cocked the hammer, and with a cataclysmic crack of epic echoing velocity that reverberated through the empty desert and in between the mountains, a bullet ripped through the barrel just spinning and I saw it spin almost in slow motion as it went forward and then immediately curved upward which shocked me completely and it zeroed in on the lizard's giant red eyeball on the right side of its face. With a squishy, sucking sound, like that of a slashed tired being ripped apart as the knife was removed from the tear in the rubber, the bullet jetted through the lizard's eye, and the ground quaked, and the lizard stopped guffawing and turned and stared at me through one working eye and another eye leaking thick purple puss that was just drooping down its face, it looked at me and said, You won, Jimmy, and then exploded and thick, hairy strands of confetti came flying out of it like fireworks, curving through the sky, flittering and squirming, and I smiled cuz I knew all along that the lizard was nothing but confetti. And that was the day the Wild West had won.

I HATE MY FUCKING LIFE

I KEEP ON TRYING

dying
dying
dying
dying
dying
im fuckin dying

just one foot after
another

————————————all 4 what?

THIS IS NOT A CRIME OF PASSION

I'VE BEEN DEPRESSED
FOR SOME TIME NOW

weeks
months
years >>>>>>>my
whole fucking life

I'm about
to do
myself
in>>>>>> maybe then someone will care

313

Not Enough

I've seen things
most people don't see.
I've experienced things
only witnessed in dreams.

Nothing you do or say
is enough to scare me away.

Don't ask me!

When in doubt read a poem by someone you hate. Read a poem by someone you admire. Write a poem about someone you hate. Admire no one. Be yourself. Emulate and copy but don't obsess and become.

When in doubt do nothing. Do everything. Be no one. Be everyone. Go outside and punch the first sucker you see in the face. Punch yourself in the face.

When in doubt suck back a loogie and let it loose on the mirror. Go outside and scream at the top of your lungs.

When in doubt read a poem by someone you love. Write a poem about someone you love.

When in doubt kill yourself, give birth, rob a bank, give to charity.

When in doubt do everything cuz if you don't the system wins.

When in doubt stand on your head and sing like you're at the opera. Sing like it's opposite day, turn words upside down and hash them out backwards.

When in doubt ... don't ask me I have no answers. I'm just a bum I'm just a king I can't sing and I can't love.

When in doubt fuck off.

1.

I sit alone
consumed by shadow
the music like a corrupt soul
oozes and gushes from
some hidden place
      of the mind

2.

the people's chatter
bustling disgusted, and I
feel separated from their
madness
    their
       insanity
          that
clips me like a hockey puck

3.

the sky is dark
lacking stars—it looks like
a big black blanket
    coming down to
    smother me
I look up and see a
pinpoint
    a dot
       one
         green
it lurks in the bleak emptiness
   makes me sad

4.

bodies
they shuffle
    when I look over
    at the giddy hustle
      the people there, scattered
are arranged differently than
the last time I chanced
    a glance
      their way

5.

I wonder—sometimes
(well, not really)
what the aliens are
thinking about
      what embraces them
      do they crave
      the things that
      make them tick
fly off the handle
how can
        I make them pissed
          >>at me
        if only it was
THAT simple

6.

the painting on the
big brick wall behind
the center street alley
comes to life

when you look at it just right
        just right

    it peels off the wall
    comes down
      splashes like
      shattering glass
a stark understanding—a dark
    realization, fat and mean
    strong and lean ::: murderous hopeless
      stuck on a futile track
      taking you into the black void—

the last thing on earth that beats
and shines bright like the sun
    churning chemically twisted, and I
decide just now to give up the sickness
and branch out
    if
      only
it wasn't so damn hard
and your own heart beat and throbbed
in tune and rhythm with my own
    like an actual human being
    apart of something beyond me
    so that I wouldn't feel so alone
      anymore....

 My Demons

I'm mentally twisted, morally sadistic, but I got a touch as soft as sand, as gentle as a dandelion as the breeze brushes through and knocks the petals loose and they explode like dust. My thoughts are corrupt and rotten, my insides are bitter and mean, but I'm telling you my skin is delicately sound, and as my inner voice screams for you to leave, my outer voice chides for you to come in, to come here, to join me in the sandbox to build this castle....

My demons are rattling my cage, racking chains against the thick steel bars holding them in, but I keep them at bay, neatly tucked away inside a prison of my own making, and they don't seem to bother me there....

Except when I fall asleep at night and terrifying nightmares ratchet the insides of my brain,
but then I wake up and forget it all as I go about my day...............

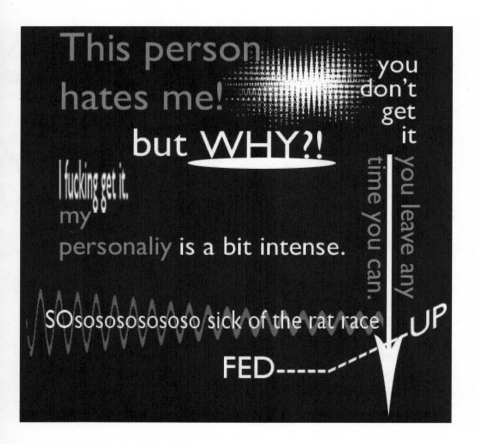

318

The lights above me
they lurk and shine.

The people around me
they lurk and spy.

I've gotta get out
of this mental maze
maybe dissipate
and go back to *yesterday* ▬

The TV promised a good life
The movies promised a
happy ending, but in this life
nothing ever ends--
it just goes on and on
swirling into madness
THIS is my madness
THIS is me
    here
            now
The only ending I know of
is in the back of a black
hearse
your body burned to ashes
and the ashes
        packed into the bottom of
a yearn
            and hurled off the bridge
            into icy waters

thats not the way I want to
go-
I do want a happy ending though
I do want some relief
but all I've got is a hand
to rub myself with as the white tears
spurt out of me
like smoke»»»»»»»»»»

321

Everything Will Always Work Out One Way or Another

(A Text Message to a Friend Who Is Having Troubles Staying Awake Throughout the Day)

I was just thinking that this issue where you can't stay awake won't be an issue 10 years from now. I think it was Einstein who said that everything with a beginning has to have an ending. And if it still is an issue, you'll have found a way to cope with it. You've been presented with a dilemma and you're going to do what all humans do when presented with a dilemma: you'll learn to adapt. Like, I get vertigo. It started when I started taking [a certain medication]. Excessive movement causes vertigo, going up and down stairs causes vertigo. If you think not being able to stay awake is rough, try getting spells of vertigo. It's scary as shit. So as a result I didn't go anywhere, I barely left my apartment cuz I was afraid of getting vertigo in public and every time I went out in public I got vertigo. That was about 3 to 4 years ago. Today I still get vertigo from time to time, but I've adapted to it. I've figured out coping mechanisms to put in place when it happens, which is very rare cuz I've also figured out ways to prevent it from happening in the first place. I was presented with a dilemma and I adapted. It took some time but that's only natural. I wanted a quick fix to solve the problem but my psychiatrist said the problem was physical and my doctor said the problem was mental. Each doctor pushed the problem onto the other. It was really frustrating but over time it just worked out.

a fate you cant escape from

thats the worst:

being buried alive w/o
your headphones to distract you
from the cold & stiff reality that is
a million little squirming maggots nibbling
on your skin

thats the worst:

your boat is going down & theres no
television set for you to watch as
the ocean overtakes your watercraft,
no movies to view as you drift away into
another world & the sea
assaults your sinking ship, boards breaking,
nuts shattering in the terrorizing waves
that come one after another

thats the worst:

when an airplane comes soaring
outta the sky heading straight to
your place of work & you left
your cellphone in your other pair of pants,
your smart phone is out of batteries
& you left the charger at home,
your tablet broke the day before,
& right now a plummeting airplane smashes
ramming & flashes as it tears thru
the glass, desks flipping & flying as the fires
are burning the whole fuckin place down

im sorry....

I don't look for trouble
trouble looks for me

I only welcome it

WAKE UP AMERICA! I'M BORED AND CRAZY, MORE OR LESS; I'M BOLD AND SOMETIMES QUITE BRAVE BUT MOSTLY I SUFFER FROM A LAZY AILMENT KNOWN AS PUTRID HEART DISEASE. IT MEANS MY HEART HAS DEVELOPED CRISP CUTS ALL THROUGH ITS INNERS AND THAT HAD LEFT ME A BITTER TEENAGER, ALWAYS WANTING TO BREAK EVERYTHING AND EVERYONE THAT GOT IN MY WAY. TOSS BRICKS AT WINDOWS, I DID THAT. KICK BYSTANDERS IN THE HEAD WITH MY STEEL TOES, I DID THAT TOO. I WAS MAD AND DISORDERED, BUT TODAY, AFTER FIXING MYSLEF TO A MULTITUDE OF DIFFERENT FORMULAS TO EXTINGUISH THIS DISEASE, I FOUND A SOLUTION— — —WHICH IS KNOWN AS ART AND ARTISTIC CREATION. I'M STILL A HATEFUL MUTANT BUT TODAY I'VE DIRECTED MY RAGE AT A PIECE OF PAPER. INSTEAD OF THROWING BRICKS AT PASSING CARS I THROW DOWN CHUNKS OF PAINT ACROSS A LARGE CANVAS WITH JAGGES EDGES AND INSTEAD OF FIGHTING FOR MY KICKS I WRITE AND THINK AND PRODUCE AND THINK AND BECOME SOMETHING BETTER STRONGER AND FASTER THAT MIGHT WANNA KICK YOUR ASS AT TIMES; BUT IT'S ONLY AS A RESULT OF THIS PUTRID HEART DISEASE, BUT WHAT I REALLY NEED TO DO IS DESTROY A PIECE OF PAPER WITH CRISP PEN STROKES AND MAKE SOMETHING OUT OF NOTHING AND TODAY I CAN FLY IF I SET MY MIND TO IT— — —SEE WHAT I DID THERE?

326

Sometimes to really enjoy art one has to let go of form and what they know about the craft; they have to leave their preconceived notions about what it SHOULD be like at the door in order to truly grasp what the artist is trying to do. Art is not about following rules, or at least it isn't for me. The reason for the level of crassness is because these are all very deep thoughts and ideas but I'm showing them in a crude setting, kind of as an ironic statement. Like, scholars dress in suits and ties and carry around briefcases, but me, I carry my luggage in a ratty old backpack, wearing filthy clothes, with fucked-up teeth and tattooed skin, but still, I can think about stuff on a deep level, too. I don't need the makeup and the plastic to think, all I need is a mind that doesn't seem to ever quit. If that makes sense. So I remove formalities such as grammar and show it at its rawest level.

Insightful Segment from
Chaos Writing:

We Live and Then We Die

Life is a joke if you ask me. Life is ugly, life is rotten, life brings all batches of disappointment when you least expect it, and when you do expect it, it gives you something you don't expect, something even worse, like a kick to the nuts when you had expected a punch to the face. That's life for you. It's a terrible terrible thing, and yet,   I haven't died yet, I'm still here, and I refuse—simply refuse—to go on living with my head in the sand, a passive bystander who gets slapped in the face, smiles through the pain, and says, "Thank you, may I have another."

NO I CANNOT DO THAT.

It's not in my DNA to sit back and let life happen to me; I must make it happen, I must stand up and take charge and kick some fuckin ass, cuz if I don't life will kick my fuckin ass....
Not That It Hasn't Already

An older woman and a younger woman, as though I'm sandwiched between their two separate ages, were just praising me on Facebook in a stream of comments following a post by a woman who HATES me....

I can't possibly imagine what she might think when she finally checks her Facebook page and receives a long rap-sheet of notifications alluding to THIS.

Just thinking about it makes the hairs on the back of my neck rise ... like we're in for a surprise of epic, and rather hysterical, proportion.

THE world falling into DAMNATION

What is your crime?

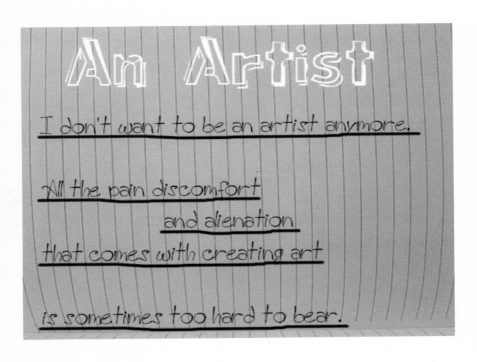

An Artist

I don't want to be an artist anymore.

All the pain discomfort
                and alienation
that comes with creating art

is sometimes too hard to bear.

Fuck Shit Cunt

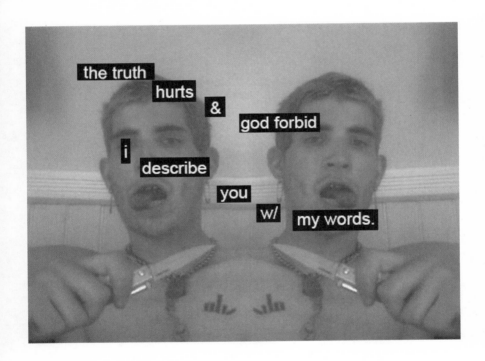

I'm so ~~ANGRY~~

right   now.

I wanna DESTROY something
I wanna destroy you.

I wanna PUNCH holes in windows.
I wanna punch holes in you.

SCREAM   SLASM   AND SMASH

AN OUTLAW

AN OUTLAW

AN OUTLAW

At an AA meeting just now ...

an open discussion

I raised my hand to share ...

the chairperson gives the room a once-over

his eyes swept right past me

my hand is the only one raised

sweeps his eyes across the room once again

and I could see the reluctancy

when he finally called my name

5 to 10 minutes left now

my hand is raised   his eyes sweep past me

he closes the meeting

Walking through this world is like walking through a hallway lined on both sides with differently shaped funhouse mirrors.

A great man once said—one of my favorite all-time American quotes—he said, "You look down at me, you see a fool. You look up at me, you see a god. You look straight at me, you see yourself."

The great man's name is

Think about it

I'm a fucking fuckup

Hey At Least I'm Somethin'

WHAT THE HELL ARE YOU????

i sit & wonder
i sit alone in the corner
i think of things i think of her
i think of the times we had
& i wonder how it all went bad.

am i the only guy in the world?
who feels this way, the only failure
of one thousand heads, one thousand
laughing faces smiling & happy
& mocking me to no end.

i hate myself i hate my life.
when i look at you its like
staring up at a giant, a big fat giant
rich & happy w/ a happy wife
& an even happier life
that reminds me ive got nothing & ill
always have nothing until i die.

i bite the tear-soaked barrel.
i bite it & i pray to something.
i ask to see the light before its too late.
i put pressure on the trigger which feels tight
in my grip, tight & hard & my last saving grace.

i hope you cry when i die
i hope your tears form a puddle on the ground
i hope you miss me & i hope ill never know
how much you cared.............

i hope i dont haveta live
to see a new day, i hope i can
work up the courage to finally do it
so for once i cud succeed in something

& i wont haveta die a failure.

STAND UP FOR THE PEOPLE THAT YOU HATE!

because without opposition we'd be a sick society.

SPARK Plug

I want to create.
I want to inspire.
I want to create inspiration

all the while punching a devastatingly volatile hole through the sound waves, destroying the noise barriers, the oh so familiar OH MY GODs and NO YOU DIDNTs and blah blah blah, the Kardashian crap that fills the mainstream media with its ignorant jargon, its popular nuances, that cut like a corkscrewing jackknife as it rams right through your fuckin heart—I will not sugarcoat a reality that cuts the old grease from beneath your beat-up jeep like Diet Coke—it's SICK, and I want to kick it off a cliff into icy waters infested with piranhas and blood-thirsty tigers....

Why don't you go suck a big fat floppy donkey dick,

said he.

The cop replied:

You know, maybe I will.

See, not all cops are so bad.

Dudes
& Dudettes

this one's for you.

idle poetry

sometimes my writing
has a mind of its own & it rises
from the page
swirling like a tornado of words,
gray & ghostly,
rising
higher higher higher,
& grasps the reader by his/her ears,
then stops spinning &
drops back into the page—
  a death-defying plunge, w/
  the reader in tow, delving
  deeper deeper deeper
  into the madness that is
  my writing

until

the reader is immersed
in my words....   HA!

gniitirw ym semitemos
sesir ti & nwo sti fo dnim a sah
egap eht morf
,sdrow fo odanrot a ekil gnilriws
,yltsohg & yarg
gnisir
,rehgih rehgih rehgih
,srae reh/sih yb redaer eht spsarg &
& gninnips spots neht
—egap eht otni kcab spord
/w ,egnulp gniyfed-htaed a
gnivled ,wot ni redaer eht
repeed repeed repeed
si taht ssendam eht otni
gnitirw ym

litnu

desremmi si redaer eht
HA!   ....sdrow ym ni

no point

no point
no point

no point
there's no point

Aaaaaaaaaaa

aaaaaaaaaaaa

aaaaaaaaaaaa

aaaaaaaaaaaa

aaaaaaaaaaaaa
aaaaaaaaaaaaa
aaaaaaaaaaaaa
aaaaaaaaaaaaa
aaaaaaaaaaaaa

smash

smash

smash

smash

smash

smash

smash

Oh Woe Is Me

Nothing's happening. I think for a trivial solution, I'm losing my mind to this thing called life. I'm bored, I need a hobby. I write the pain away—oh woe is me. Slam-dunk anxiety creeping into me—oh woe is me. I'm climbing through filth overtaking me my worrying is endless I'm cramped—oh woe is me. My mind is stretched, my mental state is broken broken breaking down. I think ... stretching out on the floor, I feel broken, I need something more, I feel troublesome and worried and depleted and ohmygod reality is slipping I'm going to sleep.

Insightful Segment from
Chaos Writing:

On Poetry

So, poetry, why is it a crapshoot? (I'm not entirely sure I'm even using the word "crapshoot" correctly though.) Because it's easy. At least for me it is. Poems don't need to make sense, they're mostly just a series of words, a series of sentences, a series of stanzas, randomly ordered in a verbal array of nonsense. I mean, some poems have meaning, and in some poems, even, the poet intended for there to be meaning. But great poetry doesn't have to have any meaning at all, that's what makes them great, I suppose. A well-written poem has depth, whether or not the poet intended it. So anyone can write a poem, and there are so many different kinds that anyone can find one suitable for their own style of writing. They can be abstract, surreal, or based in reality; they can be meaningful, meaningless, or just plain retarded; they can rhyme, but they don't have to rhyme.

That said, since you can easily cater your poem to your own particular style of writing, deeming a poem as good or bad is utterly impossible. That's why it's a crapshoot.

Although for the record, I have nothing against poetry; I think it's a great way to express oneself, because it's so easy anyone can do it.

What do I gotta do to get you
to know who I am?
Who do I gotta fuck to get you
to see me as a man?
Who do I gotta please
who do I gotta see
who do I gotta be
for you to take me seriously?

——— Jeremy Void

What is wrong with me? I second-guess myself way too much. Why can't I just be confident in every fucking thing I do, like I used to be? Why do I have to overthink every fucking move I make? too worried about what others will think, too worried about how they'll assess me, the diagnoseses they'll give me. Why can't I just be me and let go of the outcome? I used to be confident in the words I used, never apologetic for the lines I spewed, always speaking with my head high and my middle finger ready to rise up if you had a problem with it. That was the man I used to be, and today I'm a boy who is never sure, always uncertain of everything I do. I hate my brain and I hate the things I say and I hate every single line that leaves my mouth and the first thing I wanna do after speaking is say, I'm sorry, I didn't mean it like that. I'm sorry if you took it that way. I'm sorry I spoke my mind. I refuse to censor myself but I am so sorry for that fact. As my ex-girlfriend would always say, If you're sorry, you wouldn't keep making the same mistake. Like, if I was sorry for not censoring myself I should censor myself the next time instead of repeating the same derelict act in question. But I *am* sorry, I'm so sorry you have no idea. I just can't control myself, I shoot from the hip because in the moment I feel it's the right thing to say, but after the fact, it's like, SHIT SHIT SHIT, I STUCK MY FUCKING FOOT IN MY MOUTH AGAIN. The story of my life.

I know I shouldn't do it.
                    But I'm gonna do it anyway.
Fuck the results. Fuck the outcome.
                    It's all the same

                                        anyway.

The consequences are set in stone;
                    they're a fate
                            I don't want

but I know is coming, and
it's coming fast.
                    Why avoid it?
                    Why resist?
        Why not submit and give in?
                            Why do that when I can do this?
Living in shit is a dream   I've always sought after,
        and the shit came quicker than I could ask for.
I lived it,
                    I was it,
                    and

                                        I hated it.

Someone messaged me, said they find the photo I posted to be annoying and distasteful, "Will you please take it down," so I wrote "I don't know who you are" and "All my photos are annoying and distasteful," but apparently she blocked me before I even had a chance to respond. Still haven't uncovered who she is, though.

Do it again
Just 1 more time

I'm sitting in a crowd, of a few old men, they talk but I don't hear what they say. Their minds like eyes, their eyes like spies, their voices cold as ice and sharp as a knife. I sit here in this great world and wonder things that only the drunken cloaked woman lurking in the dark and dank shadows can understand, comprehend, and she scoffs and scowls in that bleak tone that sounds like a revving motorcycle as the angry rider kicks the pedal and cranks the handles.

This is my life, coming to terms with nothing, trying to understand something, learning anything my small mind can comprehend with its midget legs and arms of a giant that reach and reach and reach but the legs are too stubby and they get stuck in cement and the arms keep reaching and reaching but my brain feels heavy and I give up and go to sleep instead.

This foreign world seems so ordinary to me, like been there done that, and yet it feels so different and I find myself on an indifferent playing field, wanting something more but something seems to bore me and I find my mind slipping as my eyes cease up and I fall asleep in the shower as the plummeting spray bounces off the edge of my skull and the tub is closing in on me fast, getting tighter and the lights are brightening and opening holes in my head so as to spray me with this relentless kind of knowledge that seems almost insufferable and I pray to no one asking for relief. But then the relief comes to me unexpectedly and I look up at the clouds, the churning, shifting, and spurning webs of fluffy fog that puff out and fold over, and I marvel at the magical undulations of the spacious skies and for once this life makes a little more sense to me and that something that lurks up there comes into focus and I find satisfaction in such a bleak world and I walk away with my head upright
only to get shot down around the corner by a jagged spike of lightning that came from below and that seems to be the story of my life.

So I'm sitting in a crowd of a few old men, listening to their chatter come like waves of sonic might and I hear their voices which sound like churning rice and I watch and observe, basking in the wisdom of a thousand years of abuse, absorbing the worldly trinkets of information that seem quite foreign but still so ordinary and I think to myself, This is life, this is good, and for once I understand what it means to be bad and I understand the crashing collision of stumbling over a bed of rocks and stones and ruts and that precious bite as the rocks rip into my skin and for once in my horrible existence I see the glorifying truth and I'm falling and I'm wondering plummeting and crashing into stacks of romantic bliss and I'm not looking back. And I'm having a blast. And I'm running from the law with my one-eyed widowed girlfriend who holds a knife to my back. It's over I know.

It's over and my whole life has just begun....

Mindless

Can you imagine never asking questions?
Can you imagine being a drone,
                programmed to obey?

I'm watching people and they
all look the same, so put together,
living such a boring existence.
        I wonder,
        honestly,
        what it must be like
to be mindless.
        I wonder,
        honestly,
        why the human race
is so damned foolish, so
        futile.

And it's such a shame!
        that things are this way.

One of My Earliest Memories:

I was sick

my mom fed me some baby Tylenol
you know, the recommended dose
and then I asked:
"Can I have more?"

My mom said no

and when asked she went on to explain:
"Because then when you need it, it won't work."

And that's how I lived my life:
always needing more of any- and everything that
made me feel better than how I was already feeling.

Recovered Poem from 2011

I fell for her & all her tricks
I should've known she's a junky bitch
The life you choose is the life you got
The life I got ain't the life I want
No turning back on the way you act
But I know I'm right & that's a fact
Got hatred flowing through my veins
Love is a dream that's so insane
Tried it once and a few times after
Guess I'm insane cuz I'm the bastard

Wednesday, November 30, 2011

with 11 days sober

It's really fucking cold in here. I want to get high right now. I found out about a new drug on the market. I want to try it, just once. What could possibly go wrong? Everything, [my sponsor] thinks. For fuck's sake, it's legal, and it doesn't show up in piss tests. I'm one-hundred percent positive nothing could go wrong, but I think I'll listen to someone else for a change. Every part of my being wants to get high. I was at an NA meeting earlier today, and I was one-hundred percent honest when I said I don't want to get high. Now, I'm one-hundred percent positive I do want to get high, but, like I said, I'm usually wrong. I'm not always wrong, but for the most part, I am; so I'll listen to someone else for a change.

The Adventure Begins

no time

i wont let go.
im afraid time will pass me
too fast that ill be blinded
by its ongoing rush.
activities
events
flings
& the rest
i avoid so i dont get
swept up in the flurry
in the buzz
in the hustle
so that ill die
before ever having really been alive.
so i wont let go.

not in this lifetime....................

I had everything I could have ever wanted.

Which was absolutely nothing.

I was happier then
I was happier then life was simpler
I was happier then life was simpler
I was happier then life was simpler
then life was simpler

Beware!

Beware!

Fists full of hate
Eyes full of rage
A knife in the back
has got me locked in a cage
Scream to the world
But nobody cares
Running in circles
so you better beware

Beware of the ghost
Beware of the hoax
Beware of the boy
who will stab you in the throat

364

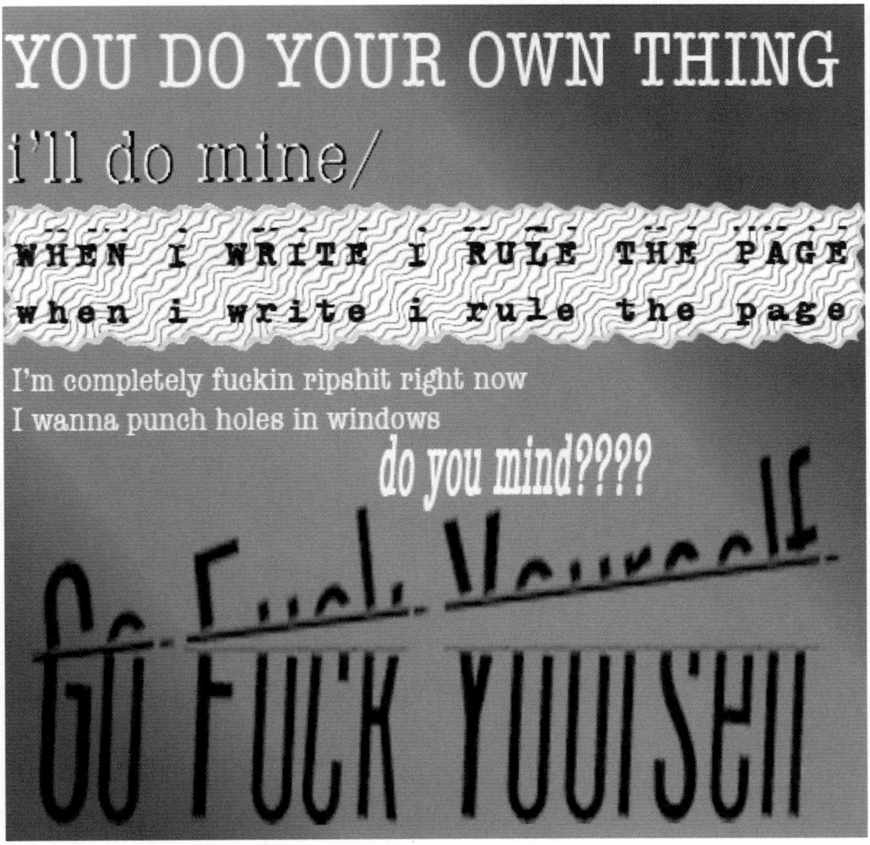

YOU DO YOUR OWN THING

i'll do mine/

WHEN I WRITE I RULE THE PAGE
when i write i rule the page

I'm completely fuckin ripshit right now
I wanna punch holes in windows

do you mind????

Go Fuck Yourself

GO FUCK YOURSELF

time&time
again
I got this
I thought I knew
I thought I knew
what I was doing>
I got this
only to prove that I didn't.
I got this
I got this
my pride
is damaged demented
I thought I had this

Little Derelict

A CACOPHONY
A COCOON I SIT IN
THE DISARRAY
IT WRAPS ME UP AND TRIES
TO SMOTHER ME DOWN.

I'M INNOCENT. I'M BRIGHT.
WILL I SURVIVE THE NIGHT
WITHOUT TRYING TO START A FIGHT?
I DON'T KNOW, I'M LOST
FALLING INTO YOUR ARMS.
YOU'D CATCH ME, BUT THEN YOU'D
DROP ME, KICK ME, HIT ME
TILL I BLEED.
I'D PLEAD FOR YOU TO STOP
BUT TO BE HONEST
I KINDA LIKE IT
MAKES ME FEEL NICE AND RAW
LIKE AN ANIMAL IN THE WRONG.

I CREEP BEHIND THE CITY
IN THE BACKSTREETS, LINGERING IN
DERELICT TAVERNS.
THESE ARE MY PEOPLE, BUT
THEY HATE ME, BUT
THEY DON'T KNOW ME, BUT
I'M TOTALLY DERANGED.

I SEE THE FIRES BURNING
I'M LEARNING TO LOVE
BUT I CAN'T STOP THIS HATE
COURSING THROUGH MY BRAIN.

IT'S ROUGH AND TWISTED
IT TREATS ME LIKE A BITCH
BUT THEN I LICK IT
I SAY GIVE IT UP
GIVE IT TO ME
GIVE IT OVER BEFORE
I HAVE A FUCKING FIT

AND THEN MY KNEES GIVE OUT
AND THE FLOOR BREAKS MY FALL
——OUCH!

Tradition is lame.
Let's all get together and do
what our ancestors have done.

Burn witches on the stake.

Junky Pride

I'm an escape artist
guess you could say
always escaping the present with
the drugs that I take
             always
                     on the run from
reality the real world everything
you've come to know and love.

It's sad I know
sad so to resent living so
damned much.

I'm scared I'm scared.
The world spins with
             or without
                     me existing .... it goes on
on and on and on, and I
just can't take it anymore
             so I run and I make
quite the living doing so.

Marketing the nightmare
and others   they laugh at
what I've been through
the fetes that I've crossed.
They laugh like it's all
just a joke   and it is
             just a joke
a silly thing that I've created.

A creation that costs
the world to uphold.
A project that consists of
endless projections that make
me sick to no end.

I run with the best
sink with the worst.
Drowning in oblivion as
I steal second base out
from under you, my friend.

We frolic in shit and
we live sickly falling apart
falling to death.... A sick sin that

it is....

We laugh in miserable droves.

When orgasms bore ya
when the world doesn't know ya
when you hate the state
and know it's gonna blowup

you wonder what for
you feel like such a whore
your middle finger sticks up on end
and life seems such a bore.

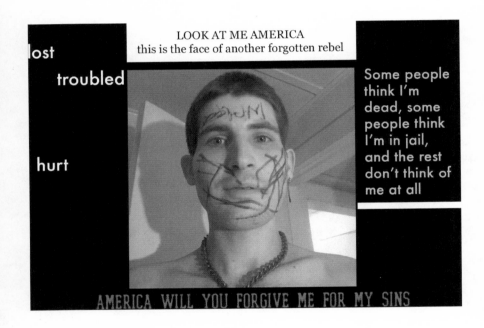

LOOK AT ME AMERICA
this is the face of another forgotten rebel

lost

troubled

hurt

Some people think I'm dead, some people think I'm in jail, and the rest don't think of me at all

AMERICA WILL YOU FORGIVE ME FOR MY SINS

Insightful Segment from
Chaos Writing:

Just Be Yourself

So that happened. Then that night I went and pissed a lot of people off. Partook in an argument with an extreme liberal cunt who calls herself an anarchist—right!—but believes picking sides is the answer. I believe picking sides is A answer but not THE answer, and that's the part she had a problem with—that I'm so indifferent to everything, so apathetic.

No, I am neither of the two, I am very helpful and very selfless and would run across the world for somebody I didn't exactly care for as a person—that's the kind of person I am——

although she didn't exactly see it that way cuz to her having no opinion is the worst stance to have. But why???? Is it really helpful to force your ideas down someone's throat? Or would it be a better use of my time if I held out my hand and asked them what was the matter. I don't know and I don't care. I do my part everyfuckingday—I even held out my hand for her when she messaged me via Facebook in the middle of the night saying she was going to kill herself....

But, as she soon figured out, *Words are my weapon, and if you piss me off, I will murder you. I COULD break it to you nicely, and I would, but if you piss me off, then I won't.*

PLAIN AND SIMPLE

I will not be victimized
I will not suffer the brunt
of your conformity
I live for one soul, one being
and it's all I need in this world.
One living creature, an overseer,
someone watching my back
looking out for number one.
I live for me and I follow
my own rules
I write my own laws
I'm the untamed cat that walks steady
on the edge of the roof without any concern///
I will only fall if it seems appropriate at the time.
Walking on the edge—not thinking but
lunging headfirst into the icy waters
is how I go about things.
I paint my world
the colors I choose to see.
I fill my life with the necessities
that I deem fit for someone like me.
So take your rotten conformity
take your rhetorical nonsense
take your colors and your slogans
take your mythical teachers
and take your rules & restrictions too
and shove em in your mouth
and swallow down your pride

cuz me
I'm still fucking alive/

A frog sat on a lilly pad. A scorpion skittered up to the pond and said, Yo, Froggy, how bout giving me a lift to the other side? But the frog said, Hell no, Mr. Scorpio, cuz if I give you a ride you might bite me and we'll both go down. The scorpion shook his head and waved his tail and said, No, I would nevah bite you, dawg. You my homie and I would nevah disrespect you like that, dawg. The frog said, Go away, Mr. Scorpio, cuz I'm not letting you on. Please leave me be or I'm dialing 911. But the scorpion scowled and spit. Tried again saying, C'mon, yo. I'm good for it and I'll even chip in for gas. But the frog stood his ground and shook his head and pointed past the scorpion to signal him to leave. This went on for a long, long time, and eventually, after lots and lots of polite chiding by the scorpion and lots and lots of intense contemplating by the frog, the squat green guy decided to let the scorpion on for a ride. The scorpion skittered on to the lilly pad and stood beside the frog, who felt rather delighted with himself for helping out the—— Then the scorpion stabbed him in the neck. The frog's vision blurred. Blood was gushing and spraying, the frog was leaping and hollering, the lilly pad was swaying and sinking, and in his final breath the frog said, Why? and the scorpion replied, Cuz I'm a scorpion!

THE BULLET

I hear the cock of the shotgun,
the click of the rifle,
the crack of the handgun;
the sound the hammer makes when it snaps the platform.

The gun fires a shot,
the powder explodes,
the sound hard and sharp,
the bullet blows out the muzzle and searches for its mark.

The target ruptures upon impact,
the bullet cuts right through,
and I see it coming and start running for my life.

The bullet is fast
and I don't think I can evade it,
but I can try,
and so I try,
and my heart hammers inside.

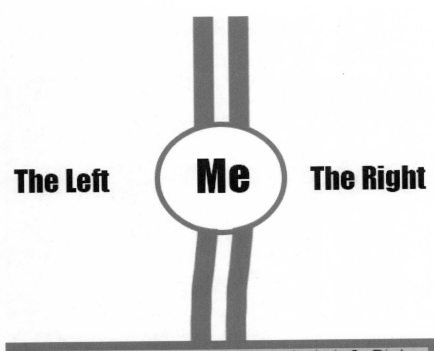

The Left   Me   The Right

If 2 friends are fighting, what do I do? Pick a side or try to find a sollution?

I am sitting in the writing group, doing a free-write. It's free, right? so I can write freely and freely I will write. My mind is like an inflating bubble, filling up with air as it rises to the sky—and then, POP!, my dreams snap out of existence like a reverse bunny-out-of-the-hat trick. It's a scary thing, right? I dream, but sometimes these idiotic notions of mine get too big for my head to contain—and then I get a headache, you know how that feels>>>>>>>>>> I get depressed, all wound up with these sappy things called feelings, until I take something, anything, to wind me down, or until I do something that takes my focus away from these prior ruminations: This person hates me this person hates me this person hates me this person—SHUT THE FUCK UP!!! Stop your fucking yapping, your voice sounds like a rapid succession of firecrackers going off in my head, just crackling and snapping and crackling and snapping, POPPOPPOP! Make it stop before I get an aneurism or something. See, this is what I do when I'm alone, stowed away in the privacy of my own home; I yell at myself, my inner dialogue which is incessantly relentless consists of constant shouting—it's traumatic, I know, and I'm the rape victim here. I still to this day have flashbacks of the devastating whip that crackled and snapped across my back, leaving a slash as bright as lava and as wide as a leering smile all the way down my ribcage. Still I remember that time when I stood outside myself, threw myself head-first into the wall, and held me there as I stole my own innocence with a series of angry, but short-lasted, thrusts. That's the shit I deal with daily, only I do it to myself, imagine that>>>>>> I'm both the victim and the victimizer. Have you ever seen the movie *Fight Club?* that's me, tenfold. Only I know, I'm aware, I understand the tremendous weight I carry around with me; I know I'm the one beating myself up, me. It's always been that way, but you know what? I prefer it like that. It's like forcefully whacking off a man twice your height and three times as wide, a man who could easily punch a hole through your head——only it's not at all like that, that's just an absurd example of what reality plus non-reality and speculation plus non-speculation and sickening ruminations that spin webs of nonsense inside my head, are doing to me. Every day I live with this burden. Now, put that in your pipe and smoke it. Maybe you'll turn into a turtle and spread your wings and lift off. Or an elephant that swims just like a panda bear, or something that tells me everything will be all right and one day I will have my way and soon enough I'll be drifting and swooping and flapping and hooting amid the rest of the colony of bats, my brethren, free to live fast and wild and free, and no silly thinking will dampen the adventure that is soon to happen here.

I notice race

black
aisian
indian
etc.   etc.

I'm not blind
and I won't pretend to be

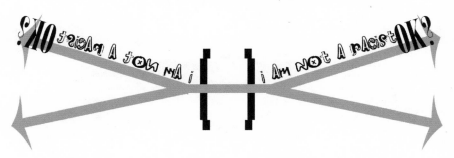

YESTERDAY

I am
better than

TODAY

I am
perfect

TOMORROW

I am
worse than

A Joke Is a Joke Is a Joke

Last night I stood onstage
told a joke that
nobody seemed to understand
and in response
they called me an asshole
said I'm an offensive prick
that I'm a bad person
I should not speak of such blasphemies
they said....

It was just a joke I told them
just a joke....

Close your eyes
cover your ears
wrap duct tape over your mouths
take a drill and drive it through
your fucking brain
don't utter certain phrases
don't discuss certain ideations

or be deemed a sadist ...
is that really what you want?

How do I tell someone that
they're stupid and their
opinion is stupid, without this
person thinking I'm stupid and
my own opinion is stupid?

This one's for you

E
a
t

M
y

S
h
i
t

I've got my own problems to deal with stop calling me I can't handle it I got problems of my own go away my problems are more pertinent not yours mine I'm sick of your complaining I'm not a shoulder to cry on I'll be your friend but if you shed one fucking tear I'll drop you so quick you wouldn't know what to do with yourself go away cuz I've got my own fucking problems these fucking problems are mine and I simply have no time for yours......................

Bother someone else
See how they like it

A Sea of Gloom

It's February
the air is warm,
the sky is blue,
& i find myself
surfing a sea of gloom.
I want to be happy
really i do, but
all i see in the forseen future
is a dim star
shining its shades of gray
all across the land
ebbing
& going black.

It's hopeless
i traipse the vaccuum
going back & forth
wondering
WHAT FOR?

I kick a stone
innertia pulls it
across the road
it hits the curb & stops,
& then it occurs to me
in my diminishing skull
that fate
has got no place for me....

Don't you laugh at me....
There's a method to my madness
a course for my action///

where you see sadness I see
growth/
where you see trouble I see
strength/
where you see insanity I see
brilliance/ I see a new way of being

I see the waning light in the madman's eyes
I see the declining heart that throbs
          deep inside the slut's chest>>>>
          behind years of neglect and abuse

I see the dried-up tears dripping beneath
the psychopath's eyes
I listen to the sun, it speaks to me....
it tells me things you would never dreams of
things you could never come to terms with
          you will die not knowing
          die ignorant and blissful
          deceased and in the heaven of the gods

as I watch the pirate ship sink and the men
on board die in the assaulting abyss

they cry and scream and fight to stay afloat
as I shed one yearning tear at the hope that
they make it to the next....
          that they carry on like bandits
          and thieves
          and bad men in the eyes of the noble

but I see a light, an evolving star, that looms
in the midst of evil, showering its iridescent glory
on the ones who choose a life of sin....

They are golden
they are great
they are the best
they are the chosen few....

They die for your sins >>>>>

Welcome to the Vicious Spiral!

Strap on your seat belts

because you are in for the ride of your life.

I AM MY OWN GREATEST CREATION, BUT THE POWER I HOLD IN
MY HANDS IS MADDENING AND I SNUFF IT OUT WITH DASTARDLY
DEEDS; I SELF-DESTRUCT AS A FORM OF PACIFICATION. THE
MIND IS A FRAGILE TOOL, AND MY MIND IS LIKE A DELICATE
FLOWER---THE SMALLEST AMOUNT OF PRESSURE IS ENOUGH TO
SET IT OFF, AND NO ONE CAN SAFELY PREDICT THE OUTCOME, IT
RUNS RAMPANT, RACING THROUGH TIME, SLINGING THOUGHTS
LIKE A FUCKIN GATLING GUN. IT'S UNSTOPPABLE, AND I SNUFF IT
OUT WITH DASTARDLY DEEDS.

THE END

People ~~IDEALS~~
$$=$$
||are||
$$=$$
~~IDEALS~~ People

Ain't it fun

when you're always on the run
when your friends despise what you've become
when you get so high that you just can't cum
when you know that you're gonna die young

such fun!!!

People are simply too concerned with their potty pissing contests to give a legitimate shit about others. I SAY Hang the assholes, hang em high, beat em with a stick until they die.

A lonely candle
in a dark room

Smash a Lightbulb
Tonight

smells putrid to
me.
It smells like
rotted fish, like
acidic dicks.
It smells like burning
fetal matter,
like lighting a bag
of dog shit and dropping it
on your neighbor's
front steps.

I don't know why
we bother lighting up
the night.
I don't know why
we cry when someone
dies.
I don't know why anyone cares,
because goodness loses its
meaning when everyone
does it.

The night is beautiful
and should thus be
preserved.
You talk about saving
lives; well
the night has feelings too.

I don't vote because
I'm ignorant.
I'm ignorant and I
prefer to keep it that
way.

DON'T
VOTE

Politics is just an
orgy, don't you
know?

I feel like in order to vote, one must take a test to
prove that he/she is up to date in world affairs

that he/she is aware of who is
fucking who///

396

I was disillusioned
my prior illusion of
      the AMERICAN DREAM
was smashed
stuffed in a blender, and I
saw a side of life most people
never see cuz theyre too busy
accepting the lie

Hey, the lie accepts them
      so why not?

But me
I saw past the lie
I had no choice
it was either that or
      get trampled by
      white men dawning blue
      suits and brandishing
      blue briefcases filled with
      paperwork//

I JUST GOT
BETTER THINGS TO DO!!!

The AMERICAN DREAM
is not what it seems
The american dream
is just not for me///

When I dream about AMERICA
the only thing I see
is red, and it fills my vision
like spilt blood
      --that's my american dream)))

397

THE STORY OF MY LIFE

Chapter 1: I was brought into sadness.

Chapter 2: I was raised into badness.

Chapter 3: I delved into madness.

Chapter 4: I sanded the rusty metal
defused the flames of hell
fought to the death with the devil
and came through with a tale to tell.

Chapter 5: I got hit by a bus.

Don't take it slow
Burning out is inevitable.
Don't take it easy
Burning out is inevitable.
The future is approaching
Burning out is inevitable.
The city is coming apart
Burning out is inevitable.
Don't stop
   don't get stale
      don't wait
         no need to yell
Burning out is inevitable.

spit on
things you
don't like!

I'm just a fatalist

I talk myself out of doing the right thing

in so many ways

because it's not like it's gonna work
out anyway, you know.

Like something good and positive will actually come
from my life. **FAT CHANCE!**
Doom and gloom is all my future has in
store for me.

I know none of this is true, but it feels so true, and my feelings have a way with words that my common sense does not have; they can twist words and bring my common sense to the same page and make it agree, thinking, You know my emotions do kind of have a point.

on the outside looking in   the crowd stands off
to my right   in a solid drove   flanking the
coolest one there   I dream of being   I
wanna be flanked   I wanna be followed   be
someone else   it makes no sense   why I'm
me   and I'm sad   and lonely, lost in
stuck in a daydream   walking thru the brain-
storm   as my head buzzes   weighed down
with   it sucks   the pressure is pushing me
back   forcing my back, my hand   holding
me down!

STOP!   this isn't   what I wanted
not quite what I expected   what it meant to be
cooooooool   I'm scared   the walls   the
crowd   the taunting sneers   all peering thru
me   like I'm made of   my skin is translucent
and slimy   I backpedal   bump into   the
locked door stops me short   mutinous people
with hearts that throb   visible in their chests....

I CAN SEE THRU *THEM*

this daydream morphs into   it shifts   and
changes   and the walls   the doors are
jammed, locking me in   I bang the steel boards
which   the walls are closing in   on me
I pace   in circles   I pace   back and
forth, straight up and down!

treacherous   trickery   it hits me like a whip
the leather   leaves a crisp, red welt across
my face stings   STOP!

the crowd conjures   laughing at me   the
laughter drills my ears, tears thu my head
the world   the walls   the locked doors
I'm twirling in place   scared   I'm search-
ing   the crowd flanks me, the walls undulate
unfolding   the laughter   hands tear at me,
claw me, my clothes ripping and   shedding beneath
the commotion!

I'm   outside the bar   on the patio   sit-
ting at a picnic table   the crowd off to my right
I watch them thru the corner of my eye.....

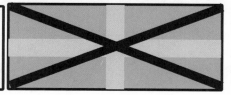

403

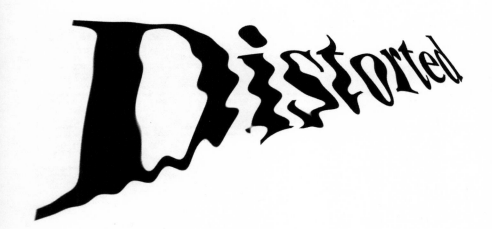

Stuff your phony religion
Stuff your sacrilegious masochistic
Phony business of this disease-ridden
garbage stricken with termites
and maggots
up
your   ass.

!!!TURN UP THE VOLUME!!!

!!!TURN UP THE VOLUME!!!

!!!TURN UP THE VOLUME!!!

!!!TURN UP THE VOLUME!!!

407

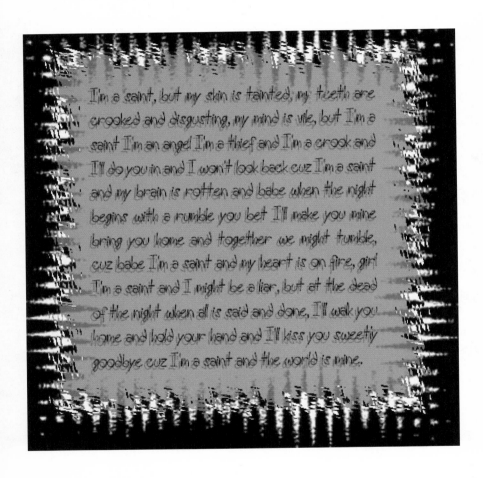

I'm a saint, but my skin is tainted, my teeth are crooked and disgusting, my mind is vile, but I'm a saint I'm an angel I'm a thief and I'm a crook and I'll do you in and I won't look back cuz I'm a saint and my brain is rotten and babe when the night begins with a rumble you bet I'll make you mine bring you home and together we might tumble, cuz babe I'm a saint and my heart is on fire, girl I'm a saint and I might be a liar, but at the dead of the night when all is said and done, I'll walk you home and hold your hand and I'll kiss you sweetly goodbye cuz I'm a saint and the world is mine.

I put on this face for people cuz I'm really not such a bad person after all, but still I have these sick thoughts that I must address and if I don't address them they will consume me. So you see, I write to keep the demons away and I'm sure people read my writing and think I'm such an asshole. They think that I'm 2-faced or whatnot. Haha, well guess what, I am 2-faced. It's very hard to coexist in such a tiny world without faking your way out of madness and pretending everything is fine and dandy. That's just reality. People would not understand, so you play the game. You pretend to be someone else.

I'm doing great. Living the nightmare and trying to find ways to market that. I wanna exploit the ex-ploiters, steal money from the rich and burn it all to the ground. Just pile it up, douse it in gaso-line, light a match, and let the flame do the rest. I wanna see the sociopathic big business men fall to their knees and ball as they watch their children perish amid billows of cigarette smoke and piles of fast food. I wanna witness the world turning in on itself, the poor getting rich and fat, and the rich getting skinny on crack. One of these days I'll turn water to wine. Treat the poor to a drink, while the rich stand on the corner panhandling for our easily swindled dough. And then I'll be doing better than great: I'll be grand, I'll feel like the man, my ego would have skyrocketed, and in a few years the rich will rise the ranks and knock me down and take my cash and force me to work as a gizz catcher at the local strip club. Every man will have their day.

411

I've overcome my problem, stepped over my dillemna like it's a dead body left out in the road. Now what?? I'm just faced with another problem, looking the next dillemna right in the eye. That's life for you: you think you got it made; well, you don't—you're just as fucked as the next guy. But that doesn't matter, I guess. We are all dying, death sits right around the corner waiting, so while we're all here:

LET'S DANCE

in between the flames

LET'S TANGO

on the dead mans grave

THIS IS MY ART, Part 2

I know my art is dark and thought provoking and maybe even scary to certain audiences, and maybe people are thinking, Is he okay? is he gonna do himself in tonight? I'm a little worried; or maybe people are thinking, What an asshole! he just wants to complain, he's only seeking attention, is all---all for a few more LIKEs. But the truth of the matter is, I like this kind of art. When I see art of a darker variety, I feel stimulated, I feel joyful and alive, I feel like I'm on top of the whole FUCKING world and I don't know why that is. I like things that bite I guess, for I've always surrounded myself with a more "dangerous" kind of person, even though to me the average Joe was rearing to bite my head off, the prom kings and queens lurking around the corner brandishing switchblades and clubs just waiting for me to come rounding the bend, and you all know what would happen to me then, right? Yeah, MY people wear spikes and leather, but YOUR people wear uggs and denim with plastic smiles and phony lives that seem so pathetic but still scare me senseless. You see, I stopped checking out plastic-looking girls one day on the train as I admired these two hot preppy-looking girls standing by the door, and then the thought popped in my head: "Like fucking a dried-out blow-up doll, your dick chafing the plastic twat in between her legs"---painful and gross, right? Well, that did it for me; those girls no longer seemed hot anymore and the kind of girls that did intrigue me had piercing scowls carved across their faces, sporting short, spikey hair, with leather jackets dashed and tainted with loads of paint and spikes and studs sticking through the vacant spaces. That's my kind of girl, this is my kind of art. Darkness doesn't seem so scary anymore when you've lived it, like walking through a haunted house; only the haunted house is your life and the ghouls and goblins hiding in the shadows getting ready to pounce on the first passerby that crosses their paths, are your friends and the only ones left to fear are the quote-unquote "normal" folk who are wanting to destroy you.

413

Not Now

I reach the breaking point
the Whole Wide World melts away
my visions blurs....
It's just me and the paper
me & the pen.
I tap the pen—there's gotta be something
for me to say
something that hasn't
been said before.

A single thought
a solid idea
something not overdone
I got this I got this
but I stare at the empty slip
and realize that I don't.

Writer's block sets in.
I'm finished. My time has come
and now it's over I'm done.
The song coming from
my stereo skips and skips
and skip-skip-skips.
My brain aches I sit here
and I've just got
nothing to say
anymore............................

I rack my mind with ideas
but it all seems just the same
as before
overplayed
overdone
over and over and it's over.
I bleed my mind
time and time again
I seek answers I plead for
something or another to put down
on this sheet of paper.

It's useless.
My time has come
and now it's gone.
My life's work unfinished
I traipse my mental dictionary
but all the words are blotted out
all my thoughts feel so
blank tonight.
It's not fair.
I'm not done I'm not done

but I am
and I place down the pen
and try something else on for size.

415

Dingy Alleyways
Dirty Floors
Roofs Looming Over a Sea of Nothing
I was there
I was there
it was dank and rough
it was mean and rotten
I was there
I was there
there was nothing to be scared of
there was no reason to avoid it

the lights were out
the shadows lurk and shift on the floor
the world as we know it
it goes topsy turvy
it flips——it flips
cavernous dwellings a pit of despair
I was there
THERE—THERE—THERE

                    Dingy Alleyways
                        Dirty Floors
Roofs Looming Over a Sea of Nothing
                          I was there
                          I was there
              it was dank and rough
             it was mean and rotten
                          I was there
                          I was there
     there was nothing to be scared of
     there was no reason to avoid it

        the world is blotted out in blackness
                      run away DARLING
                      run away DARLING
                  the things that go bump
                      the things that bite
         the things that run around at night
                   are sick and dastardly
                     ridden with disease
                  a thing to watch out for
                 cuz it will make you sick
                 IT WILL MAKE YOU SICK

                     cuz I was there....

A DREAMER, A SCHEMER, AND A FREAK

A true poet—

To be a true poet
one must walk in death's shadows
one must see the truths and learn how to spin
magnificent lies

The poet treads on the outskirts
always on the outside looking in
sometimes envious but usually
dallying in the realm of the narcissist

To be a poet
one must not forget anything
no single detail of guilt and shame
lost in a brainstorm of historical facts

The poet finds love in loveless entities
sucking down the pipe and ramming the spike
into his veins, tipping bottles and running scared
all the time. The poet thrives on misery

prospers in pain, usually self-inflicted
an existential, twisted thing that most people avoid
but for the poet it becomes god
his soul purpose
the only reason to go on

The poet's life is a lonely one
a pondering so deep it alienates himself
the poet is born to lose
a rebel with no cause, a writing devil
that spins fabricated psalms for you
and then erases them in a wisp of flames
because it will never be good enough

Solitude is the poet's only destiny
he squanders alone and searches
for someone to whom he can relate
but like everything else in the poet's life
his search turns up no results

The poet is a thief stealing hearts
stealing you but too detached to move
his own heart, it just throbs with toxic emotions

The darkness comes and the poet
sits alone in the shadows with
his pen and paper and scribbles a note
to himself:

Was it worth it?

Insightful Segment from
Chaos Writing:

Jeremy Void's System of Values

See, the first two values mentioned here—open-mindedness and genuineness—both create freedom. They help freedom grow and blossom. They help it prosper. Open-mindedness allows others to be free, and genuineness allows oneself to be free.

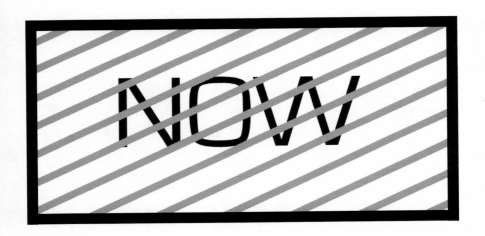

My boss yelled at me

I looked up

He was screaming

I said what?

His screams turned to shrieks

The fuck?

He didn't pause to breathe
            didn't stop to think
            didn't stop
                        period
just kept screaming

I was standing in the dining room

Everyone was watching us

I was rather confused

What the hell
was wrong with this dude?

Then he stopped
            just stopped

And in the absence of noise
            the world felt empty

and I was alone
            so alone

in the dining room surrounded by
            diners
            eating their food

They tried not to look at us
            but they were looking
            I saw them looking
            it was obvious

My boss's face was turning red
            puffing out
            like a perturbed blow fish
            in the fish tank

He lifted his finger
            started to say something
            but stopped
            just looked at me
with these beady bloodshot eyes

He looked mad
            lowered his finger
            and walked away

and I never saw him again....

422

Destroy the state

so   **the moral of THIS story**

the lesson
the moral
the key piece of information
i want you to walk away w/
is:

whether it be drunk, angry, or jus plain naked
butt naked
in the end we all crash & burn (everyone)
        in the end.... so stop worrying
about it because your worrying
will only make me late....

424

an art form

life is happening
& im dying.
or at least
i feel like im dying.
people—friends, family, neighbors
—all ebb, as i stand still.
i was the king of the hill
at one point in life
    (or at least
    thats how it felt
    to me, like i was a star
    like i was somebody
       anybody
      anybody but me at least),
but now the only stars i see
are the ones that blink out
in the sky, jus close their eyes &
go to sleep—disintegrating beauty.

i dont sleep anymore.
i stay awake all night & think
of things that make me depressed.
i tell people its to refresh those creative juices
i got boiling inside me because when i dont
sleep they boil over & spill out onto
the page.

im an artist. im lazy & weak.
im an artist, whose past was crazy
& whose future is bleak.
i wonder in vain why i didnt die
all those years ago, & i pray
oh how i pray
for that bullet to find my skull—
jus one stray bullet is all.

i know people will miss me,
      but i dont care.
now, whos the selfish one here?
i want to end my own misery
& they only want to prolong it.

the wrong place at the wrong time is really the right place at the right time in desguise. look under the fabric of dirt & grime & youll find adventure. things that are crass & gritty have more character than things that are plastic & pretty. i/d rather stand in a pile of shit than go to a famous nightclub w/ paris hilton; i/d rather rob a bank than win the lottery. i/d rather bomb a church than join one.

INTO THE MADNESS

JEREMY VOID

TONIGHT I'M GONNA SPRAYPAINT MY NAME ON THE MOON

———If I was only a foot taller, maybe an inch thinner, a bit better looking, or had a larger dick, I might feel a little bit better about being me, about being here, and living now, but truthfully I dream about being him, being there, and living then.

———If only I was smarter, had a car, and some cash that could buy me that, then I might feel more alive, feel higher, and farther, and I might want to be in these shoes, but these shoes never seem good enough.

———More hair, more muscles, more drugs, more drugs, more drugs, so I could be someone else and someone else and someone else, but that guy he's got one less leg and one less eye, and that woman is missing a tit and she's living in a shack that I'd rather not have.

If only a bomb fell I might feel better about this hell, but the bomb wasn't wide enough and didn't carry a big enough blast and now only half this country has been destroyed and it's just not good enough.

428

A man steps outside
                    side
                    side
                    side
                    side
                          sinks into the ground
                                        like

        quicksand
            sand
            sand
            sand
His life flashes before his eyes——*his eyes!*
        He thinks he's going to die!!
Overhead the sky changes.
        A flash of light sparks, and
                an idea
comes to him....
His head feels heavy, his body feels light.
He allows himself to sink
                        down
                                down
                                        down

He waits
patiently.
        He wonders
where the quicksand came
            from.
It wasn't here before, is
his final thought before
he is submerged in it.

My Brother

Junkies bite the dust, it's what they do and it's what they do best. Wasted and dilapidated, their lives dwindle and dwindle, while their friends sit in safety and watch as they fiddle with death. The reaper is rearing after you, my friend, he's got you on his list, another wasted existence, and it makes me sick as shit. You & I, we shot the shit together, we snorted shit in our noses, we popped pills and guzzled booze like it was all just some sick and twisted joke that would never fucking end. Or so we thought. Then the mallet came clanking down on the podium and they sent me away from that wasteland, and now, years later, I'm looking through a microscope that illuminates the past. I see you lost in your own madness, lost in yesterday's world, and it makes me sad to know that I brought you into this crap....

fun

fun

fun

FUN
---

fun

fun

fun

Insightful Segment from *Chaos Writing:*

You're Stupid Because You're Stupid

And then she came in with the rape-jokes argument, which eventually turned into the You're-stupid-because-you're-stupid argument.

One thing I can't stand—it's like my pet peeve—is being called stupid. Probably because all my life very few people have taken me seriously. I don't appreciate being told I am of lower intelligence than you, because chances are, you're wrong. Plain and simple. I'm very smart and tested to be in the 86 percentile in regards to IQ. Which means only 14% of America's population is tested smarter than me. And I'm getting smarter by reading all the time. So you see, I am not stupid and I don't appreciate being treated as such. Which is the number-one reason why I can't stand actual stupid people. Especially those of whom think they're smarter than they are. Know your place, is all I'm saying. Stupid people tend to use the argument: you're wrong because you're wrong. They can't argue for shit, unless you are into subjectivism, in which case their arguments do in fact hold ground. But in intelligence-ville, an argument must have objectivity. So I try to argue with them, and they always walk away feeling like the victor, thinking I'm the stupid one.

Never argue with stupid people, I say, because you'll always lose....

Like in this case, with that girl.

432

Through the Eyes of a Stranger

I sit alone,
up all night
a lucid dream like a spider
spinning webs in my head.

How do I describe me?
Someone I admire more
than anyone I've ever met.
How do I describe this man

that goes everywhere I
go and doesn't leave me alone.
This man sits here, where I sit
and this man known me better

than I know myself.
I dread his company,
only I look forward to it
and how can I exist without him.

I come here today (tonight)
to tell you about this man.
Who is he? A void, maybe,
a lost soul bringing justice

to a world unjust.

Maybe if I think in terms
of describing a stranger
the words might come
easier and I can finally tell you

about me.

A Self-Portrait

What's the difference between
0 degrees and 360 degrees?

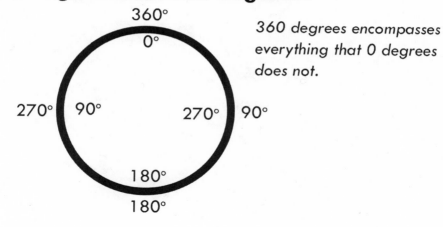

360 degrees encompasses everything that 0 degrees does not.

I got something to say.   Something I need to say.

I'm getting older and my soul is rotting. I spent a century doing things that cracked my reflection in half, and I'll spend the following centuries mending the cuts that cut me deep and make me bleed oily vile that evaporates before it hits the floor. My world is melting and I can't hold on any longer. My vision is disintegrated and my perception is derelict and the world is shattered like the mirror after I took my skateboard and ran it through the glass. I'm back where I started, only the beginning is too far out of reach, and I'm running to catch up, I'm running but I throw up the last meal I devoured, my heavenly dumpster dinner that tasted like tainted flowers. How far can I fall before the train takes me out? How far can I throw before my arm breaks and the train takes me out? How loud can I yell before my voice catches in my throat and that dastardly train takes me out? I decide I might hitch a free ride, so I'm chasing after it but it only gets farther and then it's behind me and I stop running but the very thing I'm after explodes in a thunderous, blundering, humdrum cacophony of crass clapping bats that flap and scatter up and out, and now I just don't know anymore. I'm lost, and the TV is on.

What now???

437

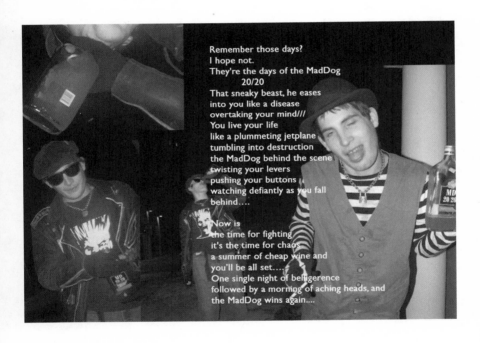

Remember those days?
I hope not.
They're the days of the MadDog
              20/20
That sneaky beast, he eases
into you like a disease
overtaking your mind///
You live your life
like a plummeting jetplane
tumbling into destruction
the MadDog behind the scene
twisting your levers
pushing your buttons
watching defiantly as you fall
behind....

Now is
the time for fighting
it's the time for chaos
a summer of cheap wine and
you'll be all set....
One single night of belligerence
followed by a morning of aching heads, and
the MadDog wins again....

438

When I was younger, but not too young I suppose, I had no problem getting girls—as easy as picking them off of trees. With a new girl every week I was. But now, at 28, things like that seem much harder, especially in a city as small as Rutland, where girls just get recycled back into the mix and you can't get away from them————
ever.
Every decent girl is taken it seems. Every good looking girl has a boyfriend and I sit and watch these couples and they never seem to break, as if they've been welded together to time and nothing is strong enough to break their hold....

IT'S FRIGHTENING

how perfect some of these couples seem to be together............

And I will never have a chance of my own to weasel my head in between these wretched developments called love and say:

WHEN'S MY TURN

THIS IS FOR ALL THE SCUMBAGS in the world.

I MASTURBATE
I CHECK OUT GIRLS TOO YOUNG FOR ME, you know the ones
I HATE EVERYTHING I DON'T UNDERSTAND
SOMETIMES I ENJOY WATCHING PEOPLE SUFFER
SOMETIMES I MAKE MYSELF SUFFER just so I don't have to feel normal anymore
I TAKE MONEY FROM THE GOVERNMENT AND USE IT TO KILL MYSELF
SLOWLY
I DO EVERYTHING IN EXCESS
I LITTER   I STEAL   I CHEAT   I LIE
I TELL PEOPLE WHAT THEY WANT TO HEAR ALL THE TIME

shall I go on?

BUT HEY, DON'T HATE ME FOR IT
I'M NO DIFFERENT THAN YOU
KEEP PUTTING ON YOUR MASKS EVERY SINGLE MORNING
KEEP TELLING YOURSELF AND YOUR FAMILY AND YOUR COWORKERS
that you are better than this
KEEP LYING AND YOU WILL DIE with the truth buried deep inside
KEEP LYING AND VEERING YOUR EYES when you face yourself in the mirror every
single morning of your useless lives
WE KNOW THE TRUTH
WE KNOW THE TRUTH
WE KNOW THE fucking TRUTH about you
because IN THE END IT'S NO USE

IT'S ALL A MATTER OF TIME!

Animosity As a Virtue

And hate isn't necessarily a bad thing. It's an agent of change. Discomfort is good for the soul, it makes you see things that happiness blinds us of, it shows us things in our life that aren't right. Hopefully the day comes when you're so uncomfortable that you make the necessary steps to get comfortable. Plus, if you loved everything, you'd be equally as sick as if you truly hated everything. There needs to be a balance. A yin and a yang. I'm sure you don't hate everything, but at times I'm sure it feels like you do. I can totally relate. On my worst days I wanna murder everyone who gets in my way, but on my best days, I wanna fuck everything that moves. See, it's okay to be angry at times, it only means you are a human being, but don't let that anger consume you. There are two wolves in our head, one for love and the other for hate, and whichever wolf we feed gets bigger and stronger and soon consumes us. So feel the hate, let yourself be hateful if that's what you need; just don't let it consume you. Punch a wall, scream as loud as you can—and fuck the neighbors if they complain—just feel what you gotta feel and it'll pass. Embrace the hate while it's there because hate is equally important to love, and fuck anyone who says you shouldn't hate....

442

You have been cordially invited

the
SELF DESTRUCTION
PARTY

One Can Hope, Right?

I was planning on bringing books with me to NY, a lot of books, as many as twenty, if I can carry that much. The reason being, I assume there will be a lot of scholars at the party, people with significant occupations, who may be able to get me on my way to success. The plan is, while inside the party I will carry up to three books at a time and leave the rest in the car and I'll try to talk up some people and see if they might know people. I'll start with, So, what do you do?—a typical conversation starter. They'll tell me, we'll talk a bit, and then they'll ask, And what do you do, my fine sir? Typical of scholars to end a phrase with "My fine sir." It's how important people talk. So I'll say, Funny that you ask. And then I'll spring my book on them like a magician picking a bunny out of a hat. Their eyes will surge open, saying, Holy shit!!! That's what their eyes will say. Keep in mind, these are scholars I'm talking about. So their eyes will say, loud and clear, Holy shit!!! You're a published author; and wine will squirt from their mouths and splatter in my face. I'll take a napkin and wipe away the liquor, while simultaneously handing over my book. Part 1 of my plan complete. Now their eyes will bulge out of their sockets and they might even piss a little. Who knows? Ultimately they'll say—I mean say, like out loud for everyone to hear—they'll say, Fucking A, you're a genius, a master of the art, one of the most magnificent authors I've ever seen. With a wave of their hands, a friend will appear. You might want to take a look at this, they'll say to their friend. He/she will reach in his/her pocket and pull out a monacle and fasten it around his/her eye, lower his/her head into the book, and then come up smiling, handing me a crisp one-million-dollar bill, and say, You got yourself a deal. Mission accomplished. Ch-ching!

It is unhealthy to agree

It is unhealthy to agree

It is unhealthy to agree

446

There's a reason it's called

Chaos

Writing

Scum of the Earth

1. He tells me I only need to pay for the gas it would take to drive me to Burlington, but then when I get in his car he wants more—enough to pay his cable bill, he says.

2. He expects me to sign him up second-to-last at the open-mike and then he'll leave and come back in the nick of time to read, missing all the other performers.

3. He's basically upset that he wasn't succesful in screwing me over.

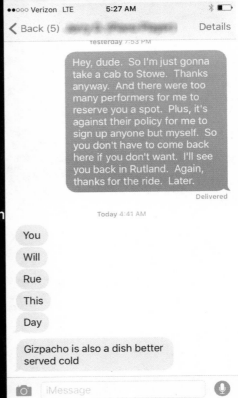

●●○○○ Verizon LTE   5:27 AM   ⚹ ■▭

‹ Back (5)   Details

Yesterday 7:53 PM

Hey, dude. So I'm just gonna take a cab to Stowe. Thanks anyway. And there were too many performers for me to reserve you a spot. Plus, it's against their policy for me to sign up anyone but myself. So you don't have to come back here if you don't want. I'll see you back in Rutland. Again, thanks for the ride. Later.

Delivered

Today 4:41 AM

You

Will

Rue

This

Day

Gizpacho is also a dish better served cold

📷   iMessage   🎤

Well, anyway, I've got things to do, images to distort,
words to shape, and truths to manipulate

Hope you enjoyed the book, cuz I
know I've enjoyed making it

FEEL FREE TO READ MORE!
to buy more!
by promptly going to www.chaoswriting.net
immediately!!!

books are available at Amazon.com too

THANK YOU

Credit Where Credit's Due

IT STARTS HERE (Pp. 1)
my old band Lethal Erection's logo

This Is Punk Rock (Pp. 17)
The Germs were probably the first Punk band in LA in 1976. Their singer, Darby Crash, who had killed himself by taking an intentional heroin overdose, was replaced by actor Shane West who played Darby Crash's roll in the biopic about him, *What We Do Is Secret*.

d. a. levy (Pp. 27)
d. a. levy is my favorite poet.

The Wrong Place at the Wrong Time (Pp. 28)
In this picture are a bunch of friends of mine from Boston.

Like Heroin to Me (Pp. 43)
"She's Like Heroin to Me" is the title of a song by the Gun Club, from their album *Fire of Love*.

Loud & Fast (Pp. 45)
"Fuck Rock & Roll" is a song by the Television, written by Richard Hell. The lyrics are: "I can't dance / I'm a bad driver / Fuck rock & roll / I like to jerk off / don't you? / Fuck rock & roll."

I wanna start an art revolution (Pp. 51)
The Chaffee Art Museum is the one and only art museum in Rutland, VT.

A Crude Writing Experiment (Pp. 82)
Pub 42 is located in downtown Rutland, VT.

keep it clean (Pp. 97)
Minor Threat is a Punk band from the early '80s.

Punish or Be Damned (Pp. 99)

"Punish or Be Damned" is the title of a song by the Screamers, from their album *Demos 1977-78*.

I'd rather see what I see (Pp. 109)

"Your world is not for me / I'd rather see what I see" is a line in the song "I'm a Raccoon" by the Briefs, from their album *Hit After Hit*.

A World of Our Own (Pp. 116)

In these pictures are me and my ex-girlfriend Julia Sorrentino.

Losing Your Mind (Pp. 121)

In this picture is a friend of mine.

From Richard Hell's "Betrayal Takes Two" (Pp. 147)

This is the second verse in the song "Betrayal Takes Two" by Richard Hell and the Voidoids, from their album *Blank Generation*.

How do you expect me to sleep at night! (Pp. 187)

This is the chorus of the song "Sleep at Night" by the Cigarettes, from their album *Will Damage Your Health*.

Sitting at the Bar (Pp. 241)

The Downtown Bar & Grill is located in downtown Rutland, VT.

Life As a Poet in RUTland, VT (Pp. 253)

The Center Street Alley is located in downtown Rutland, VT.

On Punk Rock: A Dying Culture (Pp. 270)

The Subhumans, UK Subs, and Crass are all Punk rock bands from the late '70s, early '80s.

PRETENDERS (Pp. 278)

The Buzzcocks are a Punk rock band from the late '70s, early '80s. "Everybody's happy nowadays" is a line from their song "Everybody's Happy Nowadays," from their album *Operator's Manual*.

An Animal (Pp. 329)

This is the one and only verse in the song "An Animal" by the Anti-Nowhere League, from their album *We Are the League*.

Spark Plug (Pp. 364)

Spark Plug is the name of the band I started with my friend Ryan in Rutland, VT. The point was, I would read my poetry while he added noise in the background, kind of like noise-core, in a way.

Such a Bore (Pp. 397)

In this picture is an old friend of mine, whose name I can't remember, kissing me on the cheek.

Like Heroin to Me (2) (Pp. 412)

"She's Like Heroin to Me" is the title of a song by the Gun Club, from their album *Fire of Love*. This picture is of me and my ex-girlfriend.

Ain't it fun (Pp. 422)

This is the first verse in the song "Ain't It Fun" by the Dead Boys, from their album *We Have Come for Your Children*.

360 degrees (Pp. 464)

This is something that my therapist Tomás Brown, author of *Robert's Ritual*, always says.

Scum of the Earth (Pp. 478)

This was a text message exchange with a guy I know who lives in Rutland, VT.